teach® yourself

managing your own career

teach yourself[®]

managing your own career
pat scudamore and
hilton catt

The **teach yourself** series does exactly what it says, and it works. For over 60 years, more than 40 million people have learnt over 750 subjects the **teach yourself** way, with impressive results.

be where you want to be with **teach yourself**

For UK orders: please contact Bookpoint Ltd, 130 Milton Park, Abingdon, Oxon OX14 4SB. Telephone: +44 (0) 1235 827720. Fax: +44 ((from 09.00–18.00, Mond message answering serv our website www.madab(

For USA order enquirie Customer Services, PO 0545, USA. Telephone: 1- 5645.

For Canada order enquir Ryerson Ltd., 300 Wate Canada. Telephone: 905 4

Long renowned as the au learning – with more worldwide – the *Teach Y* titles in the fields of langu computing and education

British Library Cataloguir
A catalogue record for this title is available from The British Library.

Library of Congress Catalog Card Number: 94-68413

First published in UK 1995 by Hodder Headline Plc., 338 Euston Road, London NW1 3BH

First published in US 1995 by Contemporary Books, A Division of the McGraw Hill Companies, 1 Prudential Plaza, 130 East Randolph Street, Chicago, Illinois 60601 USA

This edition published 2003.

The 'Teach Yourself' name and logo are registered trade marks of Hodder & Stoughton Ltd.

Typeset by Transet Limited, Coventry, England.
Printed in Great Britain for Hodder & Stoughton Educational, a division of Hodder Headline Ltd, 338 Euston Road, London NW1 3BH by Cox & Wyman Ltd, Reading, Berkshire.

Impression number   10 9 8 7 6 5 4 3 2 1
Year   2007 2006 2005 2004 2003

contents

There was a time not too long ago when most of us were happy to leave the managing of our careers to our employers. This is not the case today, however. An entirely different view prevails derived from an awareness that the world has changed and employers – irrespective of how paternalistic they may appear – can only deliver to a point.

What's brought about this new attitude? The great shake-outs of the 1980s and 1990s that decimated such a large part of our traditional industry base sent giant shock waves through the world of people in careers and propelled them into unknown territory – unknown as far as they were concerned because:

- Redundancy had hitherto been a largely blue-collar event.
- The stripping out of tiers of management that accompanied so many of these upheavals effectively took away career paths that had been there for years.
- Coupled with which a new breed of employer emerged on the scene – one who seemed to be saying 'Don't hold us responsible for your career. That's your business not ours.'

It was out of the uncertainty created by all this turmoil that the idea of managing your own career evolved. After all, if you could no longer rely on your employer to do the job for you, who better qualified to take on the role than you?

In this book we start by taking you through the main considerations you need to address in your capacity as boss of your own career:

- What are your aims?
- What are the chances of you realizing those aims (a) where

you work now, (b) by shopping around in the job market, or (c) by going off and working for yourself?

- What choices are open to you and how do you view those choices?
- The development plan – what qualifications, training and experience do you need to achieve your aims?
- How capable are you of taking advantage of what's there?
- How do you see risk and what's in the way of the fulfilment of your ambitions?
- What capacity do you have to take the hard knocks? How do you survive and keep going when things don't go your way?

Armed with this assessment of where you're at now, you can start to give proper consideration to your next moves – remembering at all times that:

- It's you in charge, no one else.
- It's you who keeps the plan on track and sees to it that the targets are achieved.

The central message to this book is that managing your own career is a challenging and rewarding experience. Done properly, it will take you to new highs and enable you to enjoy the freedom and flexibility that modern careers can offer. Neglected, it will set you on the path to stagnation and underachievement.

01

setting your agenda

In this chapter you will learn:

- how to define your aims
- why ambition is important
- how to set yourself free from agendas dictated by your employer.

This chapter is about aims:

- The importance of aims in the context of a self-managed career.
- Having aims with positive outcomes; not allowing yourself to be driven by grouses and distractions.
- Ambition: having aims that do justice to your talents and giving yourself the licence to dream.
- Seeing the full range of your opportunities (not setting off on agendas that are too narrow or restricted in other ways).
- Flexibility: why it's important to have aims that you can shape and bend to the circumstances; the art of the possible and being ready to take advantage of what's there.
- Ridding yourself of ideas that are baggage from the past and no longer relevant.

Aims in the context of a self-managed career

How far are you going to go in life and what does the future hold in store for you? Once upon a time you probably looked to your employer to provide you with answers to questions like these or, more likely, you simply kept your head down, did a good day's work and trusted in your employer's judgement to (a) recognize your potential, (b) come up with the right opportunities for you and (c) look after your training and development.

Having your own agenda

The main difference between this, the paternalistic model, and a self-managed career is that, with the latter, the responsibility for determining the aims and directions devolves directly onto you. While this seems straightforward enough in principle, the biggest problem in practice can be getting used to the idea. Our first case study will help to explain.

> **Case study 1: Maggie**
>
> Maggie is a sales executive with a leading health sector supplier. Six months ago, Maggie's firm was taken over by a competitor following which the sales teams of the two businesses were merged. One of the unfortunate aspects of this merger from Maggie's point of view was the abolition of the position of Sales Office Team Leader – a job for which she was being groomed. Maggie now feels she has been left with no career prospects. Since she is ambitious, she feels she has no alternative other than to look for another job.

What we read into Maggie's tale is that her original employer paid attention to people's careers and Maggie felt comfortable with the idea that she was being groomed for the next job up the ladder. In fact it would be surprising to learn that she had any other agendas apart from the one laid down by her employer. Then along came the competitor and all that was held holy by the previous regime was thrown out of the window. The result? Maggie was left high and dry with no ideas of her own to fall back on. She is now being driven out onto the job market because she feels cheated and, needless to say, this isn't good.

Problems of not having your own agenda

The lessons to draw from Maggie's case study are as follows:

- Irrespective of how well-meaning your employer appears to be, always have your own agenda – your own set of aims and your own ideas on the direction you should be taking.
- The unthinkable can happen and, sadly, it happens quite a lot in today's world. Businesses do change hands and the new people in charge don't necessarily subscribe to the old way of doing things. Similarly managements change. Chief Executives get replaced and new brooms aren't always good news for ambitious career-minded people. Be ready.
- Aims that are restricted to one job with one employer are always potential hostages to fortune (more on this later).

Maggie is typical of a lot of people who have grown up with paternalistic employers. They have always been happy to go along with their bosses' ideas. As a consequence they can come unstuck when their bosses aren't there any more.

> **Key point**
>
> While it's great your employer has got you ear-marked for a top job at some point in the future, don't let this:
>
> - become a cause for complacency;
> - distract you from the true task of managing your own career properly.
>
> Always strive to keep your own agenda i.e. separate from that of your employer. As to the top job, view it as just one of the choices open to you. You have plenty of others as we shall see.

The importance of aims

These states of aimlessness that people find themselves in are largely brought about by a failure to acknowledge that, in today's chaotic and fickle world, setting aims and directions is down to the individual.

The message here is a very simple one. Having aims is important and an essential part of managing your own career. So always allocate some of your thinking time to deciding your aims (a subject we will be looking at shortly). Don't neglect to undertake this task otherwise you will constantly find yourself in situations where you are reacting to events like new bosses, poor pay increases, rumours of redundancies and so on. Be proactive and have your ideas prepared before receiving any bad news.

Having aims with positive outcomes

Staying with Maggie for a moment, we saw how she was being driven out onto the job market by a feeling of disaffection for her new employers, i.e. an entirely negative sentiment. What this illustrates is a common flaw with a lot of people's career management: they only give it any real thought when something happens to them that's not to their liking. They react to bad, as we noted earlier, and consequently the decisions they make tend to be hastily assembled and not thought through properly. Typically they rush out onto the job market and, either with a grudge eating away at them or the fear of redundancy snapping at their heels, they take the first decent offer that comes their way. The result, in many cases, is the start of a series of sideways moves that (a) make no progress towards a defined goal and (b) run the risk of one of the moves turning out to be mistake.

Contrast this with a properly planned approach to career progression against a defined set of aims (where, for example, a high degree of selectivity is applied to any opportunities you source on the outside job market).

Grumbles and grouses

We've all got the odd moan and groan about our employers and, by and large, this is harmless and a helpful way of letting off steam. Where it becomes counterproductive, however, is where the moans and groans take over as the main driving forces behind our career decisions. Where, for example, getting a pay rise that you view as a pittance becomes the reason for you deciding to look for a new job; or where being passed over for promotion is what pushes you into a decision to change your career. Often all you need to do here is supplant the negative thought with a positive one, for example:

- 'I didn't get the salary increase I deserve' turns into 'My aim in the next twelve months is to be paid 10 per cent more than I'm paid now.'
- 'Being an auditor is a dead end job' turns into 'I plan to embark on a career in sales.'

The distinctions may seem petty but what you are in fact doing is giving yourself an aim with a positive outcome, namely, one that, once achieved, will put new dimensions on your life and move you forward in a direction which you will view as desirable. It enables you also to see that there may be more than one way of achieving your aim. For example, if you want to try a completely new career, it may not be necessary for you to take the comparatively risky step of changing employers. Your organization may be able to provide you with the opportunity of making a fresh start in a field you've never worked in before.

Notepad

As we shall see later in the book, it helps to avoid branding employers as 'good' or 'bad'. Although there are some rogues about, the truth in the vast majority of cases is that employers are well-meaning but limited in one way or another in what they can deliver. Identifying these limitations and planning your moves accordingly is all part of managing your own career.

Warning

Being driven out onto the job market by grudges and grouses (like Maggie) is usually a mistake and frequently the cause of future grief. Changing employers always introduces an element of risk and, for reasons we will be discussing more fully later in the book, you should see your job moves as desirable only if they provide *tangible gains* in terms of the advancement of your career. In short, make your job moves count for something. This is where career aims with positive outcomes will help provide you with a measuring stick against which to weigh up any job offers you receive.

Starts and stops

Another problem with grouse-driven career management is that it inevitably consists of a series of starts and stops. Your aim is to get away from employer A so you move to employer B (end of aim). Six months later you decide employer B is no better than employer A so you put yourself back on the market again (aim reinstated). The result is discontinuity. You're only active with your career management when the pain gets too much for you. In between these periods of intense activity, your big project is either forgotten or put on the back burner.

Key point

Career self-management needs to be ongoing. It needs to become part of every day – not just something you turn to occasionally and in moments of despair. There is more on this subject in the final chapter of the book.

Ambition

This is where a lot of us fall down when it comes to managing our own careers – setting ourselves aims that are way below our capabilities. Whether this arises from a misplaced sense of modesty or whether we genuinely find it hard to make a true assessment of our own talents is hard to say. Yet the fact is that there are a lot of people who set their sights too low when it comes to establishing career aims and, as a result, they underachieve.

So how good are you when it comes to your job? Are you perfect or do you have some shortcomings? In short, are you right to be having big ambitions or should you play things a little more cautiously? Finding out how others view us is never easy. The levels of frankness we engage in during daily conversations are usually tempered by concerns for the other person's feelings. Similarly, formal appraisals don't necessarily tell us a lot – whoever does the appraisal may have the same kind of problem with frankness or their judgement could be flawed; or putting you down could simply be one of their ways of keeping your expectations in check.

Giving yourself licence to dream

Since there are more problems attached to under-reaching than there are to going to the other extreme and having ambitions that are too grand, the invitation to you at this point is to allow yourself to give expression to some of your bigger dreams. Say you want to be chief executive of a major manufacturing company by the time you're 35 or you want to work for yourself and get seriously rich in the process – there's nothing wrong with having ambitions like these even if some inner voice is telling you not to be ridiculous and to get real.

Notepad

In the next chapter (Engaging with Reality) we will address the problem of matching career aims to (a) what's available and (b) what's attainable. We will also look at the importance of feedback – listening to what the world has to tell us about ourselves and incorporating it into our ideas. In short, life is a learning process and we have to fine tune our aims as we go along.

Seeing the full range of your opportunities

So, to summarize, so far we've seen that:

- A clear set of aims is the starting point for managing your own career and making a success of it.
- Not having aims is potentially dangerous in a world where no one else is willing and/or able to mark out the horizons for you.

- Aims need to have positive outcomes – they need to advance you rather than have you standing still or going backwards.
- Aims based on reacting to unfavourable events are particularly suspect.
- Career management needs to become an everyday part of your life – not something you put to one side when things are going smoothly or hand over to your bosses when they seem willing to take on the job.
- You need to have aims that do justice to your talents – you must never fall into the trap of being underambitious.

The next subject we will look at is seeing the full range of opportunities open to you – the prelude to the exercise of choice (the subject of Chapter 3).

Narrowness

If we go back to the paternalistic model, we saw that one of the snags was the restricting of career aims to what our employers could deliver. Whether this was the sum total of our potential was, to some extent, beside the point. Take, for example, the case of someone working in a family-owned business. A seat on the board, though thoroughly deserved, may not be available to such an individual simply because he/she isn't a member of the family. Similarly, an organization that has had to shed its top layer of management to cut costs in the face of global competition won't be able to offer its middle rankers much in the way of career prospects (no matter how deserving they are).

A self-managed career doesn't have these boundaries so aims can be defined in global terms (quite literally). The difficulty we noted in Maggie's case of having aims restricted to one job with one employer need not arise – and this is to the good – because, as Maggie found out, singular narrow aims such as these are all too often exposed to the ups and downs of business fortune and the waverings of corporate whim.

Not all narrowness, however, is due to people leaving the job of determining their career aims to their employers. Some of it is self-imposed. Either because of their limited experience or simply because that's the way they are, some people set goals for themselves that are far too narrow – and this sometimes links up with an earlier point regarding aims that lack ambition.

So what are the answers here?

- Be aware of having aims that are too narrowly defined.
- Get as much information as you can before you decide on any aim.
- Talk to people who are in the know. Take note of any advice they offer – even if what they're saying is not what you want to hear.
- Learn from experience. For example, if you're not having much joy with your job applications, take stock from time to time and see if the feedback is suggesting to you that your aims are too narrowly defined. Check whether what you're seeking and what the job market has to offer don't line up or only line up occasionally.

Flexibility

Given an aim that you decide for yourself, it is important not to let it become the reason for you casting your feet in cement – a guaranteed way of getting nowhere. The modern world of careers is a strange place in which you need to be nimble on your toes at all times. Flexibility is the key word here and the next case study illustrates the point.

Case study 2: Gemma

Gemma is a human resources officer with a company in the pharmaceuticals industry. Gemma's firm has recently undergone a change of chief executive. The last incumbent left rather suddenly and his replacement arrived with all sorts of ideas for cutting costs and making the business more efficient. The upshot for Gemma is that the human resources department is set to close in three months' time and her job will be made redundant.

Two weeks into her notice period Gemma receives an approach from the Operations Manager, Kay. Kay says she is looking for someone to coordinate a new product launch and Gemma came to mind (a) because of her redundancy situation and (b) because she has good administration skills. The position would only be temporary, Kay emphasizes, i.e. for the duration of the six-month period she thinks it will take to get the new product up and running. As to the longer term, Kay is unable to make any firm commitments. If the new product fails to take off then the likelihood will be of Gemma reverting to redundancy. On the other hand, if the sales forecasts are right and the targets are met, then there will be a permanent business development role for someone – with Gemma in prime position to be top contender for the post. Kay ends the meeting by suggesting to Gemma that she goes away and thinks over the proposal. Gemma thanks her and says she will, promising to get back to her by the end of the week.

Turning the matter over in her mind as she drives home from work, Gemma feels she is faced with a difficult decision. Human resources is the only career she has ever considered. Her ambition since she graduated has been to get a Human Resources Manager's job in a large company and she has been using her present job as a way of getting the necessary experience. As to a career in business development, she has never entertained the idea before. On the one hand she realizes she has little to lose by giving it a try but, on the other, it might be best to accept the redundancy then see what the outside world has got to offer her in the way of jobs in human resources.

Though she has yet to make her mind up about Kay's offer, what we are looking at here is Gemma potentially giving up the chance of escaping a redundancy situation because it involves doing something that doesn't fit in with her grand plan, namely a career that goes in a nice tidy succession of steps from one job in HR to the next until finally she gets the top job with a big company that is her ambition.

Full marks to Gemma for taking the management of her career into her own hands. Full marks too for having ideas that aren't based on one job with one company – meaning that there is life after redundancy and her career plan isn't left in tatters simply because a new chief executive has arrived on the scene. But what Gemma needs to take on board at this juncture is the importance of flexibility which, in her case, means being able to view Kay's offer in an all-round way rather than dismissing it simply on the grounds that it doesn't fit in with her current set of ideas. A career in business development may be something Gemma hasn't considered before but, who knows, she could find she likes it better than HR. What's more, she will be adding broader experience and a new range of skills to her portfolio which, in years to come, may serve her in good stead (by opening up yet more career avenues for her). The messages here are:

- Stay flexible. Don't allow your aims to become the fetters that bind you.
- View any opportunities that come your way with an open mind. Don't consider them against a preconceived set of ideas. See them instead in terms of how they might advantage you.
- See new directions as a challenge. Don't be afraid of change. It could do you good.

The art of the possible

This brings us to another important aspect of career self-management: the art of the possible – taking advantage of what's there and on offer rather than waiting for years and years for some ideal opportunity to come up. If we use Gemma as an example, the career job in HR on a par with her present position may not be available at the moment – which means that if she sticks out for this aim (and this aim alone) she is setting herself on a course for redundancy with possibly a period of unemployment to follow. If, on the other hand, she takes Kay up on her offer she:

- avoids redundancy, and
- at the same time opens up a fresh set of career options for herself.

She can, of course, carry on applying for jobs in HR – if she's so minded. In short, she has nothing to lose and everything to gain from giving the business development role a try.

Key point

One of the great things about modern careers is their diversity. No longer do you plod along a fixed path towards some predetermined destination. Instead you take advantage of whatever opportunities happen to present themselves and use your wits to make them work for you.

Perfecting the art of the possible is an important part of career self-management. Learn to go with the flow and use what's available to you as opposed to chasing hard/impossible-to-achieve objectives. Don't spend your life hammering your fists on solid brick walls when there are plenty of doors you could be going through with hardly any effort.

Warning

Equally, don't ignore your opportunities. Opportunities, remember, have a habit of knocking only once.

Baggage

It is striking, when talking to people who see themselves in career bottlenecks, just how many of them are conditioned by baggage they are carrying around from distant points in their pasts. A typical situation is illustrated by our next case study.

Case study 3: Bas

Bas graduated ten years ago with a degree in business administration. During his final year at university Bas completed a dissertation on people management in mergers, acquisitions and takeovers, and this is what fired him with the idea of getting into this field. When it came to finding a job, however, Bas discovered that the demand in mergers, acquisitions and takeovers was for people with accountancy qualifications. Bas didn't want to be an accountant (he found the idea unappealing). He tried making applications for six months then, as his funds started to run out, he drifted into a job as a sales administrator with a manufacturing company. Today Bas still works for the same firm – still in sales administration. He is, however, becoming increasingly frustrated by what he sees as being stuck in a rut. People working in the same office, with fewer qualifications, have moved on to become area account executives or, in some cases, to take up management positions. Bas's attitude to promotion is that he doesn't want it unless it moves him nearer to his cherished goal of getting into mergers, acquisitions and takeovers. This is the view he expressed to the Sales Director 18 months ago when an opportunity to lead a special projects team came up.

What we are looking at here is someone passing up decent promotion opportunities because of a fixed idea on the direction his career should be taking. The aim in this case (getting into mergers, acquisitions and takeovers) has already proved elusive and this may be because:

- he has got the wrong background, or
- the jobs are thin on the ground because mergers, acquisitions and takeovers is a very specialist field.

Of greater significance, however, is that (a) Bas is underachieving and (b) he's slipping deeper and deeper into a pit of frustration and despair. What's in the way of him moving forward? The answer is the ambition he's been carrying round since his days at university.

Cutting himself free by dumping the baggage is one solution to Bas's problems, namely forgetting about mergers, acquisitions and takeovers and getting on with his career in sales. However, there's another way of looking at this. By giving his sales administration job his best shot (by showing proper interest in it and the prospects it offers) Bas could aspire to something far better and, who knows, in the fullness of time, he might find himself dealing with mergers as part of his responsibilities as a senior sales manager.

The moral to this story is to re-examine any ambitions you've held for a long time – particularly if the ambitions are the cause of you not moving forward. Take particular note if the ambition is one that dates from a time when you had less appreciation of what the world had to offer you and what, reasonably, you could expect to achieve – for example, from a time in your life when you were in full-time education and had no work experience other than doing, say, student jobs. If the ambition is merely baggage (and based on false preconceptions of what life is all about) then dump it – fast. Whatever you do, don't let it interfere with your ability to think freely or become the cause of you underachieving.

Questions and answers

Too old to have aims

Q *I'm 56. Three years ago I was made redundant from a senior management position in a large company and since then the only work I have been able to find is doing short-term consultancy assignments at a fraction of my previous salary. My question is 'Am I too old to have aims?' Or is it a case of being over 50 and having to accept whatever I can get?*

A You're never too old to have aims and, in many ways, the need for you to manage your own career effectively is greater now than in the days when you were safe and comfortable in your senior management job. Take, for example, the consultancy assignments. Can you make these work for you in a better way? Can you do anything to improve the level at which you are being remunerated (a) by shopping around providers of short-term assignments, or (b) by setting yourself up freelance and selling your services direct? The point here is that these are all aims and, by marshalling your thinking power, you can start to work out ways of achieving them. A further point is that your career doesn't come to a stop because you've had a stroke of bad luck. Think past the problem. Look at what lies beyond. The landscape may appear different but, by taking a positive and flexible approach to it, you will soon start to see all sorts of interesting possibilities opening up. Chapter 3 deals with choices. Believe us, at 56 you've got plenty.

Don't need to manage my own career

Q *I work for what you would describe as a paternalistic employer though I would personally not choose to use the term. My company is committed to people and their development – for example, I have a two-year career plan that takes me through a succession of secondments, at the end of which I will be appointed to my first management post at one of our six operating bases. All the time this is going on I have access to a mentor and an in-house career counselling centre. Why should I be worrying about managing my own career when the job is being done perfectly well for me?*

A You miss the point. What we are saying is that you should have your own agenda (always) and that your agenda should be separate from that of your employer. This will ensure that you view your career in its full context and not just in terms of the opportunities that your employer can provide. Irrespective of how well meaning they are, leaving your career decisions entirely in the hands of others is dangerous, as we have sought to point out. Not only do you incur the risk of narrowness, but you are also exposed to changes in corporate attitudes of the kind that Maggie experienced in case study 1. As to your nice employers, stick with them for as long as it's in your interests to do so. By having your own agenda you will be able to discern when your interests and those of your employers no longer line up. This is the point at which you start to look at what other choices are available to you.

The art of the possible – changing job functions looks bad on your CV

Q *Taking Gemma (case study 2) as an example, the next time she applies for a job in human resources management, won't the time she spends in business development look bad on her CV? At worst, won't it look like a lack of commitment to working in human resources management?*

A Increasingly, careers don't follow nice tidy patterns so periods of time spent in completely unrelated fields are becoming more and more commonplace. More to the point, evidence of wider business experience and a greater range of skills would be viewed as a plus point by most readers of CVs. In short, the answer is 'no'.

Summary

Deciding aims can be a difficult and daunting task for anyone who's never had to do it before and this applies particularly to people who've never had to manage their own careers – typically people who've spent great chunks of their lives working for large paternalistic employers who've effectively done all the thinking for them.

But left to their own devices, the same people often find themselves lapsing into two extremes of conduct and both can be equally dangerous:

- First, there is proceeding with no aims, namely a state of drifting through working life. Here you resemble a ship with no engine and no steering – you go nowhere and, sooner or later, you end up hitting the rocks.
- Second, there is inflexibility so your aims, in effect, become your bondage. In this case, the ship's steering is lashed to a fixed course that takes no account of the favourable passages or prevailing winds. Sometimes it's set in the wrong direction altogether.

Because you are managing your own career, there is no one to point out to you the error of your ways. You are left to fathom this out for yourself. However, there is a much bigger issue here. The modern world of careers is a challenging and exciting place filled with all kinds of opportunities. At the same time, however, it can be a precarious place where, thanks to global competition and the onward march of technology, no one's job is safe in the way it was 20 or 30 years ago. The only way to deal with this diversity and uncertainty is to be clear at all times about what you are seeking to achieve. To do this you need to:

- set yourself aims and seek ways of achieving them;
- go with the flow and, using the art of the possible, take advantage of opportunities that come your way;
- look after yourself by ensuring your aims don't trap you in dead ends or project you on courses that don't make optimum use of your talents.

Great careers are no longer built on staying the course with one employer but instead on a mix-and-match approach using whatever the market for people can offer someone with your skills and talents. Sometimes it may be best to stay where you are. At other times it may be more in your interests to shop around. Or you may want to consider working for yourself or even trying your hand at a completely different career. Taking decisions such as these is what managing your own career is all about – the important point being that you don't hem yourself in and that you take full advantage of the freedom and opportunity that a self-managed career can offer.

02

engaging with reality

In this chapter you will learn:
- how to keep your ideas in tune with what the world has to offer
- how to rate employers and good career providers
- how to build on experience.

Having career aims is all well and good but what you also need to consider is whether your aims are consistent with what the real world has to offer. In short, are you engaging with reality or are you setting off in pursuit of goals that will be difficult or impossible to achieve? In this chapter we will be looking at:

- Assessing the demand for your talents and seeing who wants you out there.
- Profiling employers and looking at what they can deliver.
- Over-reaching (where you may be trying to take a step too far or too fast).
- How experience helps.

Assessing the demand for your talents

In the past you could probably have looked to your employer to assess your talents and match them to what your organization had to offer in the way of career opportunities. With a self-managed career, however, you have to look after this task yourself – and it's not always easy. The next case study shows why.

Case study 4: Maxine

Maxine is a design engineer working for a company which manufactures mechanical handling equipment for the food processing and packaging industry. This is a position she has held for the last seven years (since she graduated from university with a mechanical engineering degree).

Maxine is now at a point in her career where she feels she can do something more challenging – like, for example, taking on a management role. She has had experience from time to time of heading up small teams working on projects and she finds she enjoys organizing people and their work.

The problem for Maxine, however, is that her company is small and promotion opportunities are limited. Her boss, the Design Office Manager, has been in the job for a number of years and it is unlikely that he will leave in the foreseeable future.

Feeling that the only way of realizing her ambition is to try her luck on the outside job market, Maxine has spent the last six months scanning the job ads in the local evening newspaper and applying for any interesting-looking management positions that have

---

caught her eye. To date, however, she has not enjoyed much success. She has applied for 20 positions and has not once been invited to attend an interview. Indeed, in a few cases, the firms she has applied to haven't even bothered to reply.

Maxine has already deduced that the reason for drawing a blank with her job applications is her lack of management experience. Indeed, some of the ads she replied to did actually specify that candidates must have several years' experience in a management capacity but, to Maxine's way of thinking, how is she supposed to get the experience if no one will give her a chance?

A danger for Maxine is that she will decide that there is no demand for her talents and her aspirations to get into a management job are over-ambitious. The upshot? She could get disheartened and give up.

False readings

What this case study highlights is one of the difficulties of running your own career. It leaves you to decide whether you're engaging with reality or not – in Maxine's case, deciding whether going after a management job is something she ought to be doing or whether it's over-reaching and trying to take a step too far or too fast.

So the evidence Maxine has so far is hardly encouraging. She has chalked up 20 failed job applications including some where the employers haven't even bothered to reply. But what is this flagging up? Is it suggesting that Maxine is over-reaching or could there be some other explanation for her lack of success?

A relative novice to the job market like Maxine might not yet be in a position to appreciate that:

• Competition for good jobs is tough.
• Competition for good jobs that have been advertised is even tougher.
• Preference will always be given to candidates with experience. (Employers rarely take chances when employing people for top positions. They go instead for those who can offer a proven track record.)
• The job market isn't always nice to you (employers don't always reply to your applications).

Key point

Beware these false readings because they could lead you into abandoning your project before it has got off the ground. The job market is notorious for giving false readings and we will be returning to this theme later in the book.

The message to Maxine is not to be put off by the rejections and to keep going with her applications because she could strike lucky one day and find an employer who is prepared to give her a chance – even though it may take time. She also needs to consider:

- The much easier route of making a sideways move, such as using her experience to get another job as a design engineer, except this time to pick an employer who can offer more in the way of promotion prospects.
- Whether she may have more joy by networking her way into a management job (using people she knows to effect the right introductions).
- Whether she has been too hasty in writing off her present employer as a provider of career opportunities. Could it be, for example, that her boss is being lined up for promotion? If so, could it open up a slot for her?

Profiling employers

The process of engaging with reality starts by looking at employers and seeing:

- what they're capable of delivering; and
- whether this is compatible with what you're seeking to achieve.

The exercise we're about to embark on is called *profiling*. Its purpose is to establish whether you stand any chance of realizing your career aims with particular employers or whether – because of limitations at their end – you would be largely banging your head on a brick wall.

Let's take two examples – two bright young people with big ambitions for themselves.

> ### Example A: Paul
>
> Paul is a quantity surveyor in a construction company specializing in small housing developments. Paul's ambition is to work on big commercial projects such as landmark office buildings and shopping malls.

> ### Example B: Yasmin
>
> Yasmin is a young account executive working for a highly successful advertising agency that has tripled its client base in the last five years. Yasmin's ambition is to follow in the footsteps of one of her colleagues and become a partner in the agency.

Taking Yasmin first, her ambition would seem on the face of it to be realizable. The agency is growing and the path she wants to follow is one that a colleague has gone along before – proof at least that it is there.

Paul, on the other hand, would seem to have a problem. His company isn't in the market for big commercial projects, hence what he wants and what they can offer seem to be at odds with one another. The signal to Paul? Short of selling his bosses on a complete overhaul of the company's marketing strategy, Paul doesn't seem to have much hope of realizing his ambition with this employer and any effort he expends in this direction will be largely pointless.

> ### Key point
>
> Simple though these examples are, they focus attention on the responsibility you have as the manager of your own career for ensuring that you're working for the right employer. 'Right' in this context means an employer who can deliver whatever it is you are seeking to achieve.

Profiling benchmarks

What criteria should you use when you come to do a profiling exercise on an employer? As a career provider, what separates one employer from another?

Size

There are big firms and little firms and others that fall somewhere in between. On the face of it, big firms have more to offer in the way of promotion prospects and career diversity than their smaller counterparts. Be careful, however, because some big firms can be very hidebound in their thinking; so, for example, if you want to do something that takes you across the corporate boundaries, you could find yourself up against all sorts of resistance. Also some big firms are highly fragmented so, in career provision terms, they amount to no more than a collection of small firms with none of the benefits normally associated with size. Added to which some small firms are excellent career providers. Therefore, don't view size as a stand-alone consideration – run it alongside other factors such as structure and culture.

Structure

Typical of the present day is the so-called 'flat' organization where tiers of management have been removed, usually to cut costs. Because of their structure, flat organizations don't offer much in the way of promotion prospects and you need to consider this factor if you work in one and you're hoping to move up the ladder.

Culture

How 'people-minded' is the organization you're profiling? Is it committed to developing employees to their full potential? Or is it only play-acting and paying lip service? If you're ambitious, top of the list of concerns will be the extent to which internal promotion is used to fill senior positions. Alternatively, are the top jobs always given to outsiders?

Functions

Some employers have divested themselves of specialist functions entirely by outsourcing them to outside service providers (e.g. pensions, human resources, credit management). Others, intent on cutting overheads, have scaled them down to mere shadows of their former selves. The relevance of this to you is if you happen to work in one of these specialist functions.

Performance

An organization that's doing well and growing is clearly going to be a better career provider than one that's struggling – underlining the fact that the best employer in the world still ultimately has to answer to the marketplace.

Security

Stemming directly from its performance is the extent to which an employer can offer security to its employees. Security is not, however, entirely to do with profitability. We all know of 'hire and fire' outfits where the job's lifespan is usually nasty, brutish and short irrespective of business performance.

People

Under this heading come considerations such as the turnover of staff. In traditional paternalistic organizations it's not unusual to find that people stay in their jobs a long time. While most employers would view low staff turnover as good (and an indicator of high levels of job satisfaction) it's not particularly helpful to ambitious younger people who are trying to work their way up the ladder. 'Promotion avenues blocked' is a reason frequently given for seeking other employment – recall Maxine in case study 4.

Pay and perks

How does an employer rate with regard to paying staff decent salaries and providing them with other benefits such as pension plans or health care schemes? Is the employer 'tight-fisted' or does it try to attract and retain the best people? Considerations such as these are important when it comes to profiling employers.

Warning

Returning to a point we noted in Chapter 1, what you are not doing with this profiling exercise is seeking to apply value judgements. Whether you view an employer as 'good' or 'bad' is to some extent immaterial and could serve to cloud the issues. Take, for example, the typical 'good' employer where everything is satisfactory and where, for this reason, no one ever leaves. The result? It's back to those blocked promotion paths and careers that end up in gridlock.

Notepad

Organizations change and, in the world we live in today, they can change very rapidly. For example, when a new chief executive arrives on the scene, the old culture can be swept away practically overnight. What was once a nice caring employer suddenly becomes a cut-throat organization where people are put last on its list of priorities. Therefore, never view profiling as a one-off exercise. Any view you form of an employer is one you should always be ready to update.

Matching profiling to career aims

The object of profiling, remember, is to see whether what you are seeking to achieve career-wise and what employers can offer are compatible. Career aims, however, vary from one person to the next as the following case study illustrates.

Case study 5: Tom, Mary, Earl, Dick and Jo

Tom, Mary, Earl, Dick and Jo make up the customer support team of a company that supplies a range of electrical goods, mainly to commercial end users. The company has enjoyed excellent growth in recent years largely thanks to investment in product development and distribution. Forecasts look extremely good and the directors have recently announced a major expansion plan which will put the business on a par with some of its biggest international competitors.

Tom is the senior of the team. He is 32 and has been with the company for seven years. His ambition is to get into management and, to this end, he has already been told that he will step up into the commercial manager's job when the current incumbent retires in two years' time.

Mary is rather different. Mary has a degree in Business Administration and she joined the company three years ago when she graduated from university. Mary is now 25 and for some time she has been feeling she is under-achieving. The work in customer support is interesting but her first love is marketing and this is something she has set her heart on getting into. The problem for Mary, however, is that the company doesn't have a marketing function. It uses a firm of outside consultants and this has been the arrangement for a number of years. Mary is aware that Tom's job as senior will be vacant when he is promoted and she knows that she is next in line to step into his shoes.

Earl is the youngest member of the team. He is 19 and has been with the company for just six months. His last job in a retail store folded when the store's parent company announced enormous losses and made over 200 staff redundant. Earl was relieved to find another job so quickly. He is keen to impress his new colleagues and realizes that, if he fails to do so, he could find himself back on the job market again.

Dick is 58. He has been with the company for over 20 years and he has worked in a wide range of different roles. Dick has his mind fixed on retiring when he is 60. He has been paying into a private pension plan for a number of years and believes that he will be financially secure. As to the job in customer support, Dick is quite happy to come in every day and answer the phone – providing no one gives him any hassle.

Jo works part time. She is 41 and took the job eight years ago following a career break during which she had two children. Jo enjoys her work but two months ago, her husband lost his job and now they are struggling. Jo really needs to extend her hours so that she can earn more money.

Here are five people with quite different career aspirations. But can the company meet those aspirations based on what we know about them?

First Tom. Tom is ambitious but his aspirations seem to be catered for by the impending retirement of the commercial manager. In short, Tom's ambitions are in line with what his company can deliver. In having these ambitions he is therefore quite clearly engaging with reality. As a good manager of his own career Tom must also consider that his move into management isn't entirely dependent on what his present company can offer. There are other avenues he can explore – notably the outside job market. This is important to Tom if, say, for any unforeseen reasons his promotion to commercial manager fails to materialize (e.g. the company falls on hard times and decides not to fill the post).

Let's turn next to Mary. She is an entirely different case. Mary wants to get into marketing but her company can't provide her with the opening she is looking for. What she needs to do next, therefore, is to search for other ways of realizing her ambition – for example, by seeing what other employers can offer her or perhaps looking into the possibility of working freelance. But before launching on one of these comparatively risky courses of action, it would be worth establishing whether her company would be prepared to give her a chance to do the marketing in-house by ending the arrangement with the consultants. Pursuing career aims internally is a subject we will be looking at in Chapter 7. Choices (there are always a number of ways of securing a career aim) is the subject of Chapter 3.

Moving onto Earl, job security is at the forefront of his considerations – conditioned largely by his recent experiences. Is his new employer going to be able to provide him with job security? The answer appears to be 'yes'. It is a successful business with plans for growth. There is nothing in what we know about the company to suggest that there may be a redundancy exercise in the offing. Earl, for his part, has quite rightly identified that the biggest threat to his security is if he fails to make the grade.

What about Dick? Dick is just looking for another two years' work – something the company should be able to provide.

And lastly Jo. She wants the company to let her work more hours. Will they agree to her request? With their plans for growth, there seems to be every chance. In short, this is an aim she should be able to pursue.

Thus, what we have seen here is different people with different aspirations where the company can deliver to some of them, but not all.

Over reaching

Looking at your career aims in the context of what employers can deliver is all very well, but there is another factor to consider when determining whether, in setting off in pursuit of a career aim, you are engaging with reality or not – namely you and your capability. Put simply, are you good enough or is the aim you have set for yourself over-ambitious and out of your reach?

Assessing your capability

Going back to Maxine (case study 4) you will remember that she set herself the aim of getting into management. Having come to the conclusion that she stood no chance of realizing this aim internally, she turned to the outside job market. Here she had no joy at all and, after a while, she began to think that she could be trying to take a step too far, too fast.

The point to Maxine's case study was to illustrate:

• when the judgements are down to you, just how difficult it is to know whether you're engaging with reality or not; and
• how easy it is to pick up false readings.

The problem doesn't stop here, however. To complicate matters further, your capability can be viewed differently by different people. Here is an example.

> **Case study 6: Gary**
>
> Gary works in the plastics industry. For many years Gary had a boss who told him at every appraisal interview that he didn't consider him suitable for promotion. His boss left and a new boss took his place. Within 12 months Gary was appointed to the position of Factory Manager – a job in which he has been very successful ever since. Indeed, today he is poised to take a seat on the Board.

Gary's case study is a reminder that opinions on someone's capability are only worth so much and, at the end of the day, they represent nothing more than one person's view of another. Like all subjective judgements they are potentially flawed and, as such, it is a mistake to view them in isolation. The same applies, of course, if the opinion being passed on you is that you're perfect. Take it with a pinch of salt, that's all. Particularly if the person offering the opinion stands to gain something from getting into your good books.

Under reaching

But where does this leave you? Putting to one side silly and fanciful aims (such as 'I want to be a brain surgeon' or 'I want to be chief executive of a major public company before I'm 25'), the truth of the matter is that there is a very fine line between aspirations that are within your capabilities and those that aren't. Defining this fine line is tricky and, as we saw in Chapter 1, there are some who would tackle the job of setting aims by playing safe and pitching low. To this we would reiterate that there are many more problems attached to under reaching than setting your aims too high. Notably, you could be successful in achieving your aim and find yourself in a job that's well below your capabilities. The result? You'll soon realize your mistake and then it's back to scratching your head to fathom what you've got to do to get your career back on track.

Warning

Some ideas are usually best forgotten, namely:

- ideas you have on a bad day or when the boss is giving you a hard time
- ideas that come to you on the spur of the moment
- ideas you have on holiday
- ideas that come into your head after a nice glass of wine.

Ideas such as these are rarely engaged with reality. The best ideas are usually those that evolve over a period of time.

How experience helps

Having delivered the message about false readings, we will now look at the importance of building up and learning from experience. This is yet another essential tool of career self-management: keeping your ears open for feedback and learning to incorporate what you learn into your ideas. Here is an example of someone getting it wrong.

Case study 7: Clive

Clive is an electrical technician and he works for a company that makes control panels for machinery used in the printing industry. Clive's job involves testing finished control panels and, if necessary, rectifying any faults. He has been doing this job for the last five years. He is now 29.

Clive's main problem is money. His company has never been a particularly good payer and he and his wife Zoe have decided that, if they are ever going to be able to afford some of the better things in life, he must look for something else.

Two of Clive's friends from when he served his apprenticeship now work as field service engineers. If anything, they are less well qualified than he is yet, from discussions he has had with them, he knows that they are earning far higher salaries. What's more, they are both provided with company cars.

Talking this over with Zoe, they decide that Clive should look for a job as a field service engineer. With some help from one of Zoe's friends, they put together a CV and, over the next few weeks, they send this off to six companies in the machine building industry enquiring if they have any vacancies for service engineers.

The response they receive is immediately very encouraging. Four of the six companies write back saying that, although they have no vacancies at present, they are very interested in Clive's CV and will keep it on file. With one company, however, Clive is asked to ring in straight away and arrange an interview. As the company happens to be one of the really big names in the industry Clive is especially pleased.

Two weeks later, wearing his best suit, Clive arrives for his interview. He is seen by the Service Manager who introduces himself as Mel and they spend the next half hour chatting about Clive's background. Mel then tells Clive that he has been toying with the idea of taking on a service engineer with control panel experience for some time because most of his present team are mechanically rather than electrically qualified. Clive would seem to be an ideal fit, Mel goes on to say – and this is great because it will save him from having to go through the process of advertising for someone then finding that most of the people who apply aren't suitable.

A salary is discussed which exceeds Clive's wildest dreams and, yes, there is a company vehicle along with all sorts of other perks including a private medical plan and time off if Clive wants to study for further qualifications.

It is at this point in the interview, however, that Mel drops the bombshell. The job can involve working away from home, he explains. In some cases it can mean being out of the country for several weeks on end.

Clive is taken aback. 'How often is this likely to happen?' he asks. Mel shrugs. Service is service, he explains. Service engineers have to go to the customer wherever the customer happens to be located. That's the nature of the job.

The interview ends with Clive asking Mel for a few days to think things over. He promises to get back to him with a decision by the end of the week.

Later that evening Clive has a long talk with Zoe. Clive working away from home is something neither of them have considered and he is not surprised to see Zoe's face fall when he tells her about the conversation with Mel. She is not at all happy about the prospect of being left on her own for weeks at a time and Clive can also see the knock-on effect it will have on all the leisure time activities they enjoy. In the end they decide that Clive will:

- ring Mel and turn down his offer;
- carry on applying for service engineers' jobs but make it clear in any letters he writes that he is not prepared to work away from home.

We wish Clive every success with his search for the right opportunity and, who knows, he may be lucky in finding a company that serves a strictly local market or one where the service team is divided up regionally. What is quite possible, however, is that he won't find what he is looking for because he is not engaging with reality. The reality in this case is that the nature of service engineers' jobs (servicing equipment on customers' premises) necessitates that they work away from home sometimes and for this reason stay-at-home service engineers may not be much in demand. In effect, what Clive is trying to do is dictate to the market and, not surprisingly, this rarely works.

Listening to feedback

We could perhaps criticize Clive for not quizzing his two service engineer friends more closely. From them he could presumably have found out that:

- being prepared to go where you're sent is all part of the job;
- the higher salary is probably there in part to compensate for this fact.

Other than this, Clive is doing what all of us who are managing our own careers have to do – relying to a large extent on our own experience. In Clive's case he has had an interview in which the downsides to being a service engineer have been explained to him. What he has chosen to do, however, is largely ignore this feedback and set off instead on a course of action that is rapidly veering away from reality.

Incorporating feedback into your ideas

Managing your own career effectively means:

- listening to any feedback you receive and using it to your advantage;
- not closing off this important source of learning about yourself just because what you're hearing isn't to your liking or not in tune with your own ideas.

Conversely, what you must seek to do at all times is take positive steps to tap into the insights of others – particularly those who have wider knowledge and experience than yourself. In particular:

- you must listen carefully to anything that's said to you at occasions such as appraisal meetings;
- you must attune yourself to picking up any interesting feedback from job interviews;
- you must use your networks i.e. anyone who you can trust among your circle of colleagues and contacts who can provide you with input on what is within your range of capabilities.

Key point

Don't think you know it all. Listen to others. They can often offer valuable advice on whether your ideas are engaging with reality or not.

In Clive's case, the feedback from the interview with Mel might suggest a number of possible options:

- Carrying on with his job applications but in the knowledge that he is chasing what could be a fairly narrow range of jobs (service engineers' jobs that don't involve stays away from home); realizing that, because of these limitations, his job search could take time; realizing too that he could be faced with a lot of 'sorry but no' letters and steeling himself for the feeling of discouragement this could bring.
- Developing a few other ideas – for example, what other occupations do his knowledge and skills lend themselves to? Are these occupations that he could do without having to be away from home?
- If money is the only reason for seeking a move, exploring the possibilities of negotiating a pay rise for himself.

Notepad

There is another of our books in the Teach Yourself series that deals with negotiating a better salary: *Teach Yourself Getting a Pay Rise*.

Warning

In real life, you will need more than the feedback from one interview to determine whether you're engaging with reality or not. Someone like Mel could be a one-off and, if your experience of the job market is limited like Clive's, you will have no way of knowing this. Learn therefore to listen out for messages that have familiar rings to them: opinions that seem to be shared by a number of different people.

Questions and answers

Profiling external employers

Q *Profiling an employer you work for seems straightforward enough but what if you're seeking to fulfil your ambitions by shopping around on the outside job market? How do you go about profiling an employer you don't really know?*

A The short answer is you do the best you can. You've usually got a rough idea, for example, of whether the company you're applying to is small or large. By asking a few questions at an interview or by putting out feelers among your contacts, you can usually supplement this information to some extent. However, the real point is this: you're clearly in danger of hitting a brick wall if the employer you're trying to talk into paying you a big salary in excess of the market rate is a notorious poor payer. So the message is to put your effort where it's most likely to get most success.

Boss putting me down

Q *Whether it's because of his warped personality or not, my boss seems to get a kick out of putting me down. At my last appraisal interview, for example, he told me that my prospects for promotion were practically nil. My problem is I'm ambitious but I seem to be stuck with this person and his unfair opinions. What should I do?*

A You could always try going over his head but we know in reality that this is not as simple and straightforward as it sounds. What's more, management etiquette dictates that your boss's boss supports your boss so, faced with you, the likelihood is the two of them putting up a united front. Suggestions? What about your internal networks? Is there anyone in the company you can trust and who has the ear of the boss's boss? Could such a person tell the boss's boss what's going on? Use this strategy only if you know the boss's boss has got a sufficiently high opinion of you – high enough for it to be a matter of concern to him/her that you're not happy. Other than this, stand by to start looking for another job. By trying to pursue your quest for promotion with this particular employer you may not be engaging with reality. Read also what we've got to say in Chapter 7 abut using networking to by-pass a difficult boss.

Told at a job interview to forget my ambitions

Q   *I have worked in IT for a number of years and want to get into software training (a role for which my background and qualifications seem to be amply suited). Imagine my shock therefore when at a recent interview the person sitting on the other side of the desk told me to forget my ambition and stick to what I'm doing. How should I view a comment like this?*

A   Follow the advice in this chapter and don't get too disheartened about any one opinion (the next person to interview you could see you quite differently). Having said this, any feedback you get from interviews is potentially valuable in that it could highlight some aspect of the aims you're pursuing that requires a little fine tuning, i.e. something that, once it's done, will enhance your chances of bringing your aim to fruition. It would be of interest to learn, therefore, *why* this person felt you were so unsuitable for a job in training. Was it just an off-the-cuff remark or did he/she give a reason? If, for example, there was a suggestion that you lacked training and/or qualifications then this could indicate that you should enrol on a course before you start applying for any more jobs.

Experience and age

Q   *Is experience a question of age and, if so, are older people better at managing their own careers?*

A   Not necessarily. For example, an older person who has had a one-company career with a traditional paternalistic employer won't, as a result, have much experience of managing his or her own career. Conversely, someone younger who has known nothing else except the topsy-turvy world of modern careers, for survival reasons, will be quite accustomed to making decisions and determining the right directions.

Summary

One of the difficulties with a self-managed career is being on your own when it comes to deciding whether the aims you've set yourself are consistent with:

- what the world can offer you; and
- what you're capable of doing.

In this chapter we've encouraged you to take an open-minded view of whether you're engaging with reality or not in the following ways:

- Do not allow false readings (wrong opinions you form because you have insufficient experience) to put you off.
- Always ensure you are pursuing ambitions with employers who are capable of delivering them (don't knock your head on brick walls).
- Always listen to any feedback you get and use it to fine-tune your ideas.

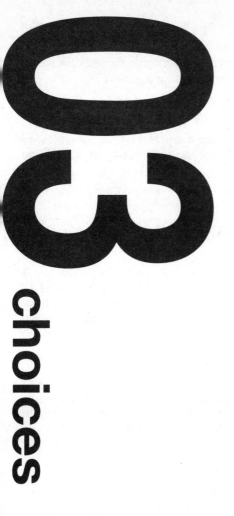

03

choices

In this chapter you will learn:
- the full extent of the opportunities open to you
- when it's right to make a move
- risk management and how to handle it.

Making a success out of managing your own career starts with choices:

- realizing you have choices (always);
- knowing how and when to exercise your choices.

In this chapter we are going to look at:

- Examining the choices open to you.
- Making moves versus staying put.
- Other choices – working for yourself; taking up short-term assignment based work; changing careers.
- Risk and how to view it.

What are your choices?

In Chapter 1 we noted a tendency among people unused to the idea of managing their own careers to define their career paths narrowly. Typically, such people fail to see the full range of opportunities open to them and we commented how, uncorrected, this kind of narrowness can lead to underachieving.

However, unfamiliarity with having to make your own career decisions is not the only reason for underachieving. Failing to see the full range of opportunities open to you can also be the result of feeling doubtful about some of the directions open to you. You could, for example, feel extremely unsure about going out and shopping the job market if you have long service with an employer or if making a move could mean losing valuable perks or that your pension rights could suffer. Here is a case study to illustrate the dilemmas some people face when it comes to determining their career choices.

Case study 8: Alice

Alice works as a Secretary/PA for a large property development company – a job she has been in for the last ten years. Following a slump in the property market, Alice's company has been through difficult times recently and one of the side-effects of this is that no one has had a salary increase for the last 18 months. To make matters worse one of the other Secretary/PAs wasn't replaced when she left so Alice is now effectively doing the work of two people – meaning she is working longer hours for which she is paid no extra.

Alice is a breadwinner (a single parent with two children still in full-time education). The way she sees her situation is as follows. Her pay is falling behind what she thinks she can earn as a Secretary/PA and she feels that having to work another 8–10 hours a week without any financial recognition is unfair. However, the alternative as she sees it is going out and finding another job and, frankly, this concerns her. Not only would it be a step into the unknown but also she has to consider that redundancy lists are often decided on the basis of 'last in, first out', so from a security point of view she feels she is far better off staying where she is. What Alice can't risk under any circumstances is ending up out of work. The household budget is tight enough as it is and she was planning to use the little bit of money she'd saved up to make sure she and the children had a decent holiday this year.

Here we have someone who feels she has no choices because she is not in a position to take risks. In her view, all she can do is put up with the low pay and the long hours in the hope that, at some point in the future, her employer will recognize her plight and take steps to deal with it. The prospect for Alice? Sadly, she will probably be locked into her low pay/long hours situation for a long time to come.

Notepad

The link between choices and what people see as their capacity to take risks is one we shall be looking at shortly.

Exploring your choices

From what we know of Alice, what she is seeking is simply a fair day's pay for a fair day's work without putting her family's livelihood at risk. The hours she is being asked to do don't, in themselves, seem to be causing a problem and what we are led to believe is that she would be happy with the longer hours providing her overall package took account of them.

So what are the choices open to Alice?

• For a start she could be putting her case before her bosses. In Chapter 7 we will be looking at the business of pursuing aims and getting results within the context of a self-managed career. There you will be learning about **silent bargaining power** – the leverage you can exert in order to get your employers to give you what you want.

- Alice is right to be wary of the risks attached to swapping jobs. At the same time, however, there are ways of minimizing these risks and avoiding bad moves. The message? Don't let job hunting frighten you. Instead, learn to get good at it.

- What about splitting her hours and doing two part-time jobs? That way she would be spreading her risk across two employers (the chances of both of them making her redundant at the same time would appear to be extremely remote). With the added employment protection now available to part-timers, splitting your hours in this way no longer has to be done at the expense of curtailing your employment rights. A further advantage here is that the pay for part time work is usually based on the number of hours you do so unpaid hours tend not to be a consideration.

- She could have a go at working freelance – setting herself up as a one-woman business and building up a network of clients. That way she would largely be determining her own hours and earnings. Risky? It could be but a lot depends on what Alice has in the way of contacts and potential sources of work. (More on working freelance shortly.)

- Is there anything else Alice could do with her skills and experience – anything better paid? For example, could she look at teaching word-processing – in other words, a complete change of career? (Another subject we will be looking at shortly.)

We could continue with this list but the point here is to show that people like Alice who see themselves as 'boxed in' usually have much more than they think in the way of choices.

Key point

When you feel you have no choices think past the problem. The world of work is richer and more diverse than it's ever been, so somewhere out there is a whole range of opportunities ready and waiting for you. All you have to do is bend your mind a little and – whatever you do – never feel you're stuck with something you're not happy with.

Looking at choices can have an immediate therapeutic effect. Straight away you feel a lot better when you realize you aren't trapped in some awful job situation that you hate.

Structuring your choices

Given the range and freedom that goes with deciding your own path and managing your own career, what you must do next is decide which of your choices is the one to pursue. Here a lot depends on you. For example, if you are like Alice and constrained in the amount of risk you can take, then the best avenue to explore (at least to begin with) is the one that seems to have less in the way of downsides to worry about. In her case, this would mean starting with making her case to her bosses. If that doesn't work then she could look at her other choices – putting them in ascending order of risk (as she sees it).

Notepad

In some instances it may be best for you to explore all the choices open to you. For example, if you're out of work or your job circumstances are desperate then you will be looking for quick results. In which case, having a wide selection of 'irons in the fire' will work to your advantage.

Extending your choices

We have noted already the link between the range of choices available to you and your ability to take risks. For example, someone who is a breadwinner like Alice will feel constrained about taking a job with a new start-up business run by people they don't know, whereas someone who has no such responsibilities won't have quite the same inhibitions.

Alice is, admittedly, in a difficult position because she is the sole provider for her family and she has little in the way of savings. But let's say she had a partner with whom she could share the financial burden – someone who could take over the responsibility for looking after the family while Alice explored a wider, more risky and potentially more exciting range of choices.

What this is illustrating is simply that you can extend your range of choices by increasing your capacity to take risks. Another way of doing this is by looking at your finances and seeing to what extent you can in the short term:

- reduce your outgoings;
- tap into savings;
- engage in overdrafts and borrowings.

Key point

Try to avoid trapping yourself into job situations by following expensive lifestyles and spending every penny that you earn. Remember that you won't be able to enjoy the freedom that managing your own career offers if you're hemmed in by big mortgage repayments and bills for private school fees. Remember too those rainy days that arrive sooner or later. So don't saddle yourself with overheads and always try to keep some spare cash in the bank. We will be coming back to this subject again later in the book.

When it's right to make a move

It is increasingly unlikely these days that your career ambitions will be satisfied by staying with one employer all your working life. The reverse is increasingly becoming true in that you'll need to change jobs several times to take your career in the directions you want it to go. Indeed, staying with one employer these days often goes with stagnating and underachieving.

Warning

Intelligent planned career moves are one thing; mindless job hopping is another.

Note that too many job moves on your CV will go against you, particularly where your job moves don't appear to advance you very far. It sends the message that here is someone who finds it hard to fit in or who has perpetually itchy feet – and neither will endear you to prospective employers. What's more, job moves are intrinsically risky so, the more of them you make, the more you increase your chances of coming unstuck. So the message is:

* never make job moves for trivial or inconsequential reasons;
* make your job moves count.

Managing your own career means deciding for yourself when your career with an employer has run out of steam – deciding when it's time to get serious about looking for another job.

Stagnating

Feeling that you are in a rut is a sound enough reason for sending off a few job applications, but one of the problems facing people who are managing their own careers is *knowing* when they're in a rut (their bosses are very unlikely to tell them, that's for certain).

The difficulty is that stagnating isn't something that suddenly happens overnight. It's an insidious condition that creeps up on you over a period of time and it usually goes with spending too long working for the same employer, doing the same job.

Key point

Stagnating is dangerous. It can lead to:

- underachieving (standing still when you could be moving forwards)
- loss of confidence
- allowing your skills to lapse and become obsolete
- narrowness and only being able to see one way of doing things
- becoming resistant to change.

For these reasons you must never allow yourself to stagnate. You must take action before the condition manifests itself and the symptoms become major issues.

Stagnation is often the result of people failing to set and pursue their own agendas, that is, they're largely to blame for allowing their careers to drift into the doldrums. The answer? To wake up and get on with the task of defining their aims and then to see whether the organization they're working for is one that can deliver (the steps we covered in Chapters 1 and 2).

Opening windows on the world

One of the best ways of ensuring you're not stagnating is by keeping your faculties tuned in to what's happening in the outside world. In this way you will be able to see for yourself:

- What other employers can provide.
- Whether your salary is slipping behind.
- Whether your skills are up to date and in line with what other employers are looking for.
- Whether your perceptions are indeed becoming narrow.

How do you open these windows onto the outside world? In two ways:

- By keeping active on the job market.
- By networking with people outside your own organization – for example, people you once worked with but who have now moved on and work for other employers.

Notepad

Chapter 8 (Moving into the Future) looks in more detail at the importance of keeping in touch with what's going on in the world.

Career paths blocked

If you're ambitious and there's no way forward for you then, again, this is a reason for seeing what other employers have to offer.

Finding yourself in a career cul-de-sac tends to be associated with working in certain kinds of organizations, including:

- Organizations where, for one reason or another, staff turnover is low. Practically no one ever leaves so, as a consequence, promotion avenues become blocked.
- 'Flat' organizations where there are few layers of management hence little in the way of career ladders to climb.
- Small firms where promotion opportunities are by definition limited and where the top of the tree is often reserved for people who own a stake in the business
- Training organizations – typically organizations that take on large numbers of graduates every year in the expectation that only a few will stay long term. Here the number of people coming up the ladder vastly exceeds the number of posts available so that a promotion bottleneck develops with only a handful of people ever likely to be successful.

Key point

If your career path is blocked, don't wait to be told. See the problem for yourself and don't wait for something to turn up – usually it doesn't.

Career paths wiped out

In most cases this tends to be a spin-off from the kind of corporate restructurings that go with mergers, acquisitions and takeovers – or the arrival of new faces at the top. Typically, layers of management are taken out (resulting in flat organizations) or lines of reporting are broken up. For people sitting somewhere in the middle of all the turmoil and headcount slashing, this can often result in the next promotion step up being taken away (remember, this is what happened to Maggie in case study 1)

Being passed by

Seeing promotion opportunities that you have set your sights on being offered to others is usually a pretty strong signal that your career with an employer has run out of momentum. Be careful, however. What could be the case is that your employer has misread your ambitions because you have failed to *communicate* them correctly. Quite wrongly, they could be reading into your silence that you wouldn't be interested in taking on more responsibilities. Who's to blame if this happens? You of course.

Notepad

Chapter 7 (Getting Results) looks at the importance of making your aims known. With self-managed careers, the responsibility for doing this rests entirely on you.

Job at risk

Seeing that your job is under threat is a very strong signal to start looking around (the quicker the better). We devote the whole of Chapter 6 to the steps you need to take if you find your job is at risk.

Grievances

Feeling hard done by is another reason why people put themselves out on the job market. The premise they're working on is that someone out there can offer them something better (something more in line with their expectations). A grievance about pay is perhaps the commonest reason for people to shop around.

Warning

Earlier on, we warned you about not moving jobs for trivial or inconsequential reasons. An example we came across recently was of a woman sales manager who changed jobs because her company car was overdue for a change. She got very worked up about this, but the upshot for her was that her new job with its flashy new car lasted just six months. The moral to this tale? Think twice before quitting your job because of a grievance.

Looking to other choices

Returning to Alice in case study 8, we saw that, contrary to what she thought, she had a number of choices including some that didn't fall within the normal range that most people consider. These included:

- working for herself i.e. going freelance; and
- effecting a complete change of career by using her skills and qualifications to do something entirely different.

Working for yourself

With the exception of certain occupational groups such as journalists, working freelance was once considered to be an offbeat and potentially wayward thing to want to do. Not so today, however. People in all walks of life work freelance and you should never rule it out as far as your range of choices goes.

Outsourcing

This is worth mentioning as a lot of people get their first taste of working freelance because the activity they previously did has been outsourced. Here is an example:

Case study 9: Kuldip

Kuldip worked as a desktop publishing (DTP) specialist for a company operating a chain of cash and carry warehouses. Most of Kuldip's work was to do with sales promotions and editing and updating price lists. Kuldip did this job for four years (from leaving university with a degree in computer studies).

Just over three months ago, Kuldip's company appointed a new chief executive and, soon afterwards, there was an edict from head office announcing that certain functions within the company were to be cut and outsourced to outside suppliers. One of these functions was DTP.

Soon after this announcement Kuldip's boss Karen (the Marketing Manager) asked to see him. At this meeting Karen made it plain she wasn't very happy with the decision to outsource DTP and promised to do what she could to find Kuldip alternative employment. She said she'd heard there was a vacancy in the logistics department and undertook to put out some feelers on Kuldip's behalf. As to the DTP function, she assumed that at some stage soon she'd be told to find a firm of outside suppliers to take over Kuldip's work. She added that she had severe misgivings about moving to an outside supplier. A lot of the work Kuldip did was to very tight deadlines and in her view it would be better by far if it could continue to be done in-house.

Reflecting on this conversation afterwards, Kuldip's first reaction was that he didn't want to work in logistics. He appreciated that Karen was only trying to do her best to help him and he didn't want to appear ungrateful but DTP was a job he loved and all he'd ever wanted to do. It didn't escape him, however, that saying no to alternative offers of employment meant that he would be putting himself on the path to redundancy. Then a thought struck him. What if he became self-employed and set himself up as a one-man DTP service provider? What if he put in a tender for his old work? Next day he shared these thoughts with Karen. At first she seemed surprised he wanted to work freelance. There were downsides, she pointed out to him, like he would have to provide his own equipment and materials – plus the fact that he would be taking a risk. Kuldip countered this by saying there were upsides too. He could, for example, tender to do work for other companies and, who knows, it could lead one day to him being managing director of his own DTP business!

Asking Kuldip for time to think over his proposal, Karen's gut feeling was to give him a chance. Apart from some recognition for his good record and four years' service with the company, Karen felt distinctly more comfortable about outsourcing the work to Kuldip. After all he had proved himself reliable in the past and he knew the work and the importance of meeting deadlines. As to equipment, Karen was quite sure the company would be prepared to offer him the chance to purchase anything he needed out of his office at a knock-down price (it would soon be surplus to requirements anyway). She would have to come up with a fair way of pricing any work she put out to him but, in doing so, she would ensure that he wasn't out of pocket.

The points to highlight from this case study are the following:

- Responsible managers such as Karen are always apprehensive about outsourcing work that has previously been done in-house, particularly where the work has always been done to a good standard. At the back of their minds is the thought that with an outside supplier (unknown) the standards could lapse.
- Unintentionally perhaps, Kuldip's timing was perfect. He lost no time at all in speaking to Karen and he put forward his proposal before she had got round to contacting any outside suppliers (the art of getting in before the competition arrives).
- Karen was surprised to hear that Kuldip was happy to work freelance. From this we can deduce that she would never have raised the suggestion with him for the simple reason it would not have crossed her mind. The point here? That you need to be pro-active in these situations. It's up to you to get your face in the picture.
- Kuldip's good record was the main reason why Karen felt moved to give him a chance. She would not have been so inclined if, for example, he had been troublesome or unreliable (an aspect of the *lifelong interview* – an important lesson we will come on to later in the book).
- How companies are keen to make outsourcing work. To this end Karen is prepared to help Kuldip to set up his new business.

Key point

The critical part to going freelance is at the start when you need to get some cash coming in. It will help you enormously, therefore, if you take all or a part of your old job with you. This is the opportunity that outsourcing offers.

Sources of work

What if the outsourcing option isn't available to you, however? What if your company has no such plans?

Making a success out of working freelance depends to a large extent on being able to source sufficient work to keep your cashflow going. One of the difficulties when you start up is that you are tendering into a market where, to all practical intents and purposes, you're a complete unknown. Yes, you can build up your reputation over time, but in the critical few months at the beginning it can be very nerve-racking. Indeed, don't be too surprised if, soon after you start, you find yourself wondering if you've done the right thing.

Networking

Networking (tapping into your contacts) is an important part of managing your own career that will crop up again and again as you work through this book. Networking, however, has special significance to people who work for themselves because it's the way they source most of their work. People who use them recommend them to others, the word gets round, and so on.

But what about at the beginning? The word isn't round yet that you're the best at whatever it is you do, so how do you keep the wolf from the door till the phone starts ringing?

The answer in the case of a lot of people who go freelance is that at the start they depend to a large extent on their ex-employer. This works for them in three ways:

- They source work directly from their ex-employer, for example, helping out during peak periods in demand or filling in when someone is off sick or away on leave.
- When tendering for work with people who have never used them before and who don't know them, they use their ex-employer to put in a good word for them.
- They use their ex-employer to effect introductions.

Short-term assignment-based work

Though this didn't figure in Alice's list of choices, doing short-term assignment-based work or contracts is something that managers of their own careers may want to consider. Why do contracts? The following list gives the main reasons why people elect to go down this route:

- The money of course. Contracts pay well and, providing the gaps between contracts aren't too long, you can make a good living from them.
- If you want to work overseas, doing a contract first is a good way of dipping your toe in the water before taking the big plunge.
- Working on contracts often means you pick up skills and types of experience that are very marketable, i.e. you can use contracts as a stepping stone into a permanent job.
- Careers have their natural hiatuses – times when you feel that you don't want to throw yourself head first back into the rat race (e.g. after a redundancy). Contracts are often a good way of inserting a semi-colon into your life.
- You can do contracts when there's nothing else around – for example, during a slump.
- A contract is often a good way of filling in between jobs.

> **Notepad**
>
> Some people make a career out of working contracts. The lifestyle suits them and, in most cases, they do it for the money.

How to get contracts

Contracts are often advertised (e.g. in newspapers, professional journals, trade publications and on websites). Many overseas postings are one- or two-year contracts.

Other than this, firms of consultants are often the best source of contracts – for example, contract design offices. Some professional associations act as clearing houses for contracts.

> **Warning**
>
> Contracts can and do dry up. If you're like Alice, therefore, and if a regular uninterrupted source of income is important to you then contracts may not be the answer for you.

Changing careers

People who change their careers fall into two categories:

- Those who do it because they see the career change as a way to something 'better' – for example, more opportunities for advancement, a life with fewer complications, to escape from a career that has become boring, etc. We call these **visionary** career changes.

- Those whose hands are **forced** – for example, people whose careers have come to an end because of the decline of an industry or because breakthroughs in technology have rendered their career obsolete. Also into the category of forced career changes come people who, for one reason or another, are no longer able to do what they once did – for example, a professional sports person who sustains an injury or a globe-trotting business executive who, through the death of a partner, now has sole responsibility for the care of a young family.

Key point

If you are putting a change of careers onto your list of choices, it is important to define which of these two categories you fit into because it will determine:

- what you need to consider; and
- the best way to proceed.

Visionary career changes

This is where you definitely need to make sure that you are engaging with reality – i.e. that the new career that you've set your sights on will offer what you think it is going to offer. Here is an example:

Case study 10: Trudi

Trudi is a 23-year-old mathematics graduate who works as a statistical analyst for a market research company. She has been doing this job for the last 18 months, but she finds it boring and unchallenging. What Trudi has now set her sights on is a job in human resources management because she likes and gets on well with people.

Is Trudi engaging with reality? It's hard to say, but clearly she needs to consider the following points:

- If liking people and getting on well with them is the right reason for wanting to be a human resources manager. How would she feel, for example, if she had to make someone redundant or issue them with a warning? The point here is that the reality of jobs is often not how they appear to outsiders.
- Is she qualified to be a human resources manager? Does she need to include in her considerations the time and cost of getting an appropriate professional qualification?
- How her earnings might suffer from going back to being a learner. Whether a drop in pay is something she has thought through carefully enough.
- Whether the idea is a fad and something she has only turned to because of her disenchantment with her present job.

Key point

Visionary career changes need to be thought through properly and in the light of as many facts as you can possibly assemble. This includes talking to people who are in the career you've set your sights on and finding out what it really entails. It also means doing some heart-searching on the less appealing aspects of making a career change – for example taking a drop in salary or having to go back to college to get further qualifications. Once you've gone through these stops and checks you can proceed with your visionary career change.

Forced career changes

The rules here are very different because by making the change you have nothing to lose. The writing is on the wall as far as your present career is concerned so you're in a no-choice situation. However, you need to realize that with a forced career change time is always against you. You need to get results quickly and therefore to open up as many options as possible, by which we mean pursuing more than one choice of career. Try to draw up a list of options and apply your efforts to each of them.

> **Key point**
>
> As part of the process of exploring career changes identify your **transferable talents**, i.e. skills, experiences etc., that would lend themselves to other walks of life. If we return to Alice (case study 8) we noted:
>
> - how word processing was one of her skills as a Secretary/PA;
> - how this skill was one she could transfer into teaching.

> **Notepad**
>
> If changing careers figures in your choices you may be interested to read another of our books in this series: *Teach Yourself Making Successful Career Changes*.

Risk

Earlier in this chapter we saw how concerns over risk served to put the brake on some people's aspirations. We saw how, in Alice's case, concerns over the risks attached to moving jobs caused her to have reservations about including this in her range of options. She figured quite rightly that in a new job she would be 'last in', potentially putting her top of the list if the need arose to make redundancies. It may have crossed her mind also that she would be at risk if, for any reasons, she didn't 'fit in' (the fear of taking a step into the unknown).

Risk assessment

As the manager of your own career one of the tasks allotted to you is to carry out a proper **risk assessment** on any of the choices you are considering. Is it a safe and sensible direction for you to go in or is it one that is fraught with danger?

This is where a lot of people, understandably, get 'cold feet' – because the consequences of making bad choices can be very frightening. If, for example, you go freelance and find it doesn't work out you could end up with debts to pay off (the money you've borrowed from the bank to set yourself up). If you make a bad job move you could be faced with having to make a hasty exit and then having to take the first alternative offer that comes along. It could take several years to get your career back on track.

Upsides and downsides

However, this is in effect doing half a risk assessment, looking entirely at the downsides and failing to appreciate that any risk also has upsides. Taking freelancing as an example, the upsides might include:

- seeing the reward for your effort go directly into your own pocket;
- job satisfaction;
- the chance some day to grow bigger.

How you rate these upsides is very much a matter for you. For example, if you've got a burning desire to be the boss of your own business, then the last of these points will rate very highly.

Balancing the risks

Assessing the risk attached to any career choice means assessing both the upsides and the downsides, then asking yourself where the balance lies. If the downsides outweigh the upsides (i.e. if exercising the choice doesn't stand to move you forward very far) then the signal flashing at you is to stop in your tracks and go no further. If, on the other hand, the upsides look good then this is a signal to stop dithering and get on with it.

Key point

This further reinforces two points we made earlier:

- never make moves for trivial or inconsequential reasons; and
- make your moves count.

However, many people neglect to consider that there is another set of upsides and downsides – namely those attached to staying where you are. The upside in this case is sticking with the known (old familiar faces and places); the downside is continuing to underachieve, being by-passed for promotion, feeling you're getting nowhere – or whatever it was that caused you to consider your choices in the first place.

Warning

Every course of action has a downside and nothing is risk free. This bears out the old adage that trying to play perfectly safe is the most dangerous thing you can ever do.

Questions and answers

My pension rights could suffer

Q *I've been with the same employer for over 25 years and I am very conscious of the fact that I am underachieving. Mostly this reflects in my salary which is a pittance compared with what someone with my background and experience would be paid anywhere else. What worries me, though, about going out and finding another job is the effect this will have on my pension. As I understand it, my accrued rights will suffer considerably if I leave, meaning that if I decide to exercise my choices I will have to forfeit a hefty penalty. What's the answer to this?*

A   First, make sure you've got your sums right. The best way to do this is by having a chat with a reputable independent pensions adviser. Second, it sounds like your company operates a final salary scheme, in which case you should consider that if you're right (if you are underachieving), then your salary with a new employer and hence your final pension rights will be a lot better than if you stay where you are. As a footnote it sounds like you've just woken up to the idea of managing your own career. If so, don't overlook the fact that one of the choices open to you is to try to negotiate a pay rise with your present employer. Advice on how to do this is contained in later chapters where you will be learning about **silent bargaining power**. People like you with long service often find themselves viewed as part of the furniture but what they do have going for them (usually) is quite formidable stocks of silent bargaining power. What you, and others like you, need to do is learn how to use it.

Golden handcuffs

Q   *When I started with my present employer 12 months ago I received a very generous golden hello – a five figure sum which the company has the right to claw back if I leave during the first three years of my employment. The problem I face now, however, is that a new chief executive has arrived on the scene – a man whose methods I find hard to stomach. Under normal circumstances I would be firing off as many job applications as possible but, with two of my three years left to serve, I feel that I have no option other than to grin and bear it. As to the five figure sum, I'm afraid I blew it on a new car. Silly I know, but at the time I considered it my just reward for landing the job. Can you offer any advice?*

A   Golden handcuffs didn't get their name for nothing! What should you do? If you don't fancy borrowing the money to pay your company back then find another employer who will give you a golden hello. In other words use Peter to pay off Paul.

No choices because I'm too old

Q   *What choices do I have? I'm 58 and stuck in a job I took two years ago after being made redundant and which I hate.*

A   Everyone has choices, so don't write yourself off just because of your age. Instead, think positive and start by asking yourself what attributes you have that would weigh in your favour. Here are three we can think of for starters:

* you have experience;
* no one is going to view you as a fly by night;
* you probably have a network of contacts that you've built up over the years.

Straight away this opens up all sorts of possibilities – for example:

* targeting employers who are looking for a stabilizing influence (typically employers who have high staff turnover);
* using your contacts either to network your way into employment opportunities or as a source of freelance business;
* using your experience to get assignment-based work.

Note that no one will care how old you are if you're coming in to do a short-term assignment or provide a service on a freelance basis. The only criterion will be whether you can do the job or not.

Leaving job moves off my CV

Q   *I've been guilty of job hopping in the past but my answer to this is to leave some of my moves off my CV – particularly those firms where I've not lasted very long. Is there anything wrong with this?*

A   Yes, if you get found out. It will put a cloud over your relationship with your new employer and, if you're really unlucky, they might even give you the sack for providing false information. Our advice would be to come clean about your employment history because the past always has a habit of catching up with you. Employers, particularly the better ones, don't expect people to be perfect but they do expect them to be truthful.

Working freelance

Q *I'm 23, recently graduated in business studies, and I quite fancy the idea of working as a freelance consultant. I think I know my stuff – particularly when it comes to computers – and I have no qualms at all about borrowing money to set myself up. What advice would you give ?*

A Think again. Working freelance is tough (always) and even people with experience can find it daunting. What would be far better for you would be to find a regular job with a reputable employer who will provide you with proper training and support. If this sounds dull we apologize, but a far worse outcome for you would be pursuing your freelance idea then finding you come unstuck with all the attendant trauma and misery. Fine if you want to work for yourself but do it later when you've got some experience under your belt.

Concerns about working on contracts

Q *Is it true that some employers take a dim view of people who've worked on contracts? If so is it really an option that someone in a mainstream career like me should be considering?*

A True, some employers do associate people who've worked on contracts with people who are only interested in money so, yes, it can work against you particularly with employers who are looking for staff to stay with them long term. Should you steer clear of contracts for this reason? Our advice is not to rule out anything that could move you from A to B – for example, provide you with a stepping stone between two jobs. As to employers' fears, you can best overcome these by always making it clear at interviews *why* you decided to dabble in contract work. Was it to gain a wider range of experience? If so, the wider experience should only serve to make you a more attractive candidate. The real point here, however, is that you should never leave employers to draw their own conclusions. If you feel there are any potential areas of concern about anything you have done in the past you should:

- identify them;
- take steps to pre-empt them.

With the second of these points it could mean, for example, your having to introduce the reasons why you did contracts at some point in the interview. It could also mean you have to reassure an employer that you have no intention of going back to contracts.

One final point – employers are far less fuddy-duddy than they used to be about people who have stepped outside the frameworks of a conventional career. In other words, the concerns you have may not be quite so relevant today.

Summary

One of the great benefits to managing your own career is that, because you set the directions yourself, you have a wide range of choices open to you. No longer are you confined to what your employer determines. You are a free agent and you can explore every aspect of what the modern world has to offer.

In this chapter we have focused on making you aware of just how much you have available to you in the way of choices and how, with the application of a little ingenuity and mental energy, you can extend these choices even further. There are risks, yes, but we have encouraged you to make a proper assessment of risks rather than feel permanently excluded from the freedom of modern careers by fear of what might happen to you if it all goes wrong.

04

adding value to yourself

In this chapter you will learn:
- how to come up with your own training and development plan
- how to acquire a successful image
- bargaining power and how to use it.

One of the responsibilities you have as the manager of your own career is for your development and training. In this chapter we will look at:

• Putting together a development plan that's consistent with your aims: employability and assessing what it will take to move you in the directions you have chosen.

• Acquiring additional skills and qualifications: how to go about it and the difficulties that may arise when what you have planned is at variance with your employer's ideas.

• The importance of acquiring a winning image: the 'lifelong interview' and what this means for you.

• Using enhanced skills and qualifications to negotiate better deals for yourself: an introduction to silent bargaining power and the exercise of leverage.

Devising your development plan

Devising a development plan is important. In a world where you can no longer rely on your employer to look after your training and development needs, the responsibility to come up with the plan falls on you. This point, however, stretches a little further. If in your exercise of choices you're looking at career aims that go beyond what your employer can provide, then clearly you're the only one who can determine:

• what additional skills and qualifications you need to take you in the directions you have chosen;

• how to get these skills and qualifications.

Employability

This is your first checkpoint in devising your development and training plan. To what extent are your skills and qualifications in line with what the market for your particular brand of talents wants?

In the previous chapter we talked about career stagnation and warned that one of the side-effects of getting into a rut was allowing your skills to lapse and become out of date. This is a problem if you then want to get out of the rut. You try applying for jobs only to find that employers aren't very interested in what you have to offer. Take Linda, for example, who works for a small design and printing company where, thanks to the proprietor's reluctance to spend money, the computer software she is using is almost obsolete. Linda is currently looking for another job but to her dismay all the employers she has approached so far are asking for experience on software packages she is completely unfamiliar with.

Assessing your employability

The bottom line for people like Linda is that their employability is impaired by not keeping their skills up to date. Who's to blame? Linda would probably say her employer for failing to invest. Here, however, she is wrong. The failure is on her part for not picking up earlier that her skills are adrift from what the market is seeking in people.

Key point

Making sure you're employable by having an up-to-date set of skills and qualifications is an essential part of managing your career. Put yourself at an advantage when it comes to exercising your choices by having skills and qualifications that are in demand.

Notepad

People in declining industries where levels of investment have been poor often find themselves with obsolete skills. The difficulty they face is when the industry finally collapses. They're pitched out into a world that is hostile to them.

How do you assess whether your skills and qualifications are in line with what the marketplace wants? There are two ways, and we touched on them briefly in the last chapter. They are:

- **Keeping yourself active on the job market.** This means making job applications and registering with recruitment consultants (employment agencies). From these sources you will soon learn whether your skills and qualifications are in need of a brush-up.
- **Networking.** You can find out what's going on in the outside world by tapping into your contacts in other organizations. Former colleagues who are now working elsewhere are useful sources. It helps too if you are a member of a professional or trade association where you can meet and compare notes with people in a similar line of work to yourself.

Have you got all the skills and qualifications you need?

Having carried out the necessary checks to ensure that your skills and qualifications haven't slipped behind for any reason, what you need to do next is examine your aspirations and ask yourself whether you've got all the skills and qualifications you need to advance you in the direction you have chosen. Let's use another case study to see what's involved.

Case study 11: Don

Don has worked as a contracts assistant in the civil engineering industry since he left full-time education seven years ago. He is now 26 and intent on making a complete change of career. Feeling he needs to branch out into something with more prospects while at the same time using his IT skills, Don has decided on a career in computer sales. With this aim in mind, he has been taking some soundings.

Don first spoke to several people he knew in the computer business, including people who supplied his company with equipment. Here the consensus of opinion was that:

- it paid to get training with a reputable company;
- there was a lot of competition for available posts and preference was usually given to graduates.

Don was a bit dismayed to hear the latter. He'd dropped out of university after his first year due to financial pressures and never took the time out later to complete his course. Undeterred, however, he decided to press on with making some applications. The way he saw it was:

- he might just strike lucky;
- his good general knowledge of IT and his experience with contracts handling software would hopefully make up for not having a degree.

To date, Don has applied to most of the big names in computers and to a fair number of the smaller ones too. So far, no one has even invited him to attend an interview and he is beginning to suspect that his lack of qualifications is the reason why he is not having any success. Some of the advertisements he has replied to did in fact state that a degree would be an advantage.

Identifying areas of potential disadvantage

Allowing for false readings, there are some pretty strong signals flashing out to Don that he would probably have more success with his change of career if he had a degree. From his networking contacts and his job market experience what Don has identified, therefore, is an *area of potential disadvantage* – something missing from his portfolio of skills and qualifications that, if it were there, would greatly enhance his chances of moving his career in the direction he wants to go in.

Key point

Identifying areas of potential disadvantage is important because it highlights what you need to do in terms of acquiring more skills and qualifications. It also highlights where you may be failing to engage with reality by over-reaching, i.e. where by pursuing your aims you could be largely wasting your time.

As for Don, there is certainly no harm in him continuing with his job applications because there is, as he has correctly determined, always the chance that someone may take a shine to him. What he also needs to do, however, is adjust his expectations downwards; that is, to view himself in his unqualified state as an outsider and not to get too disheartened by the rejections. More importantly, he should ask himself what's standing in the way of his getting a degree. What could he do, in other words, to take away the disadvantage?

Acquiring additional skills and qualifications

So far, so good: you have identified any shortfalls in your skills and qualifications – anything that could make you a mismatch in terms of what you are aspiring to do – but now comes the difficult bit. How do you set about acquiring those missing skills and qualifications? Where do you go and who will pay for it? More to the point, when you're already working for eight to ten hours a day, how do you find the time?

Key point

Alhough there are some altruistic exceptions, don't as a general rule expect employers to fund training and development that has no direct benefit to them. Take Kate as an example. She is keen to learn about a new range of software as part of keeping her skills up to date (software her company has no plans to purchase). Kate may have some difficulty, therefore, in persuading her bosses to pay for the course and allow her to have time off work to attend.

Flexible learning

First the good news. When it comes to adding value to yourself by gaining extra skills and qualifications, today you have a far greater range of choices available to you than there has ever been. Open learning institutions, learning on line, colleges and other educational institutions prepared to tailor courses to practically anyone's needs – the opportunities are almost boundless. The message? You no longer have to rely on your employer to give you time off work to attend courses. You can pursue your training and development objectives independently and without having to seek permission from anyone. The main snag (if it can be described as such) is that you must get used to the idea of viewing the time when you're not at work as not being exclusively for social, domestic and leisure use. Putting up barriers of this kind will only serve as an impediment to you in making a success out of managing your own career.

Funding

You may be lucky and find someone who is prepared to provide the funding for your training and development plan (e.g. the kind of funding provided for retraining people who have been cast off from declining industries). However, there is a much bigger point here: as the manager of your own career you are responsible for underwriting your training and development needs, that is, as a last resort it's up to you to foot the bills.

Fully flexible finances

Making sure you have sufficient cash in the bank to pay for a short course is one thing, but where getting a further qualification involves, for example, taking a year out to go to university, there are clearly far more serious implications to consider. This is where we need to introduce you to the idea of fully flexible finances – an important principle to grasp if you are going to make a success out of managing your own career.

With the traditional model of a career it was a reasonably safe assumption that your earnings would rise in a more or less orderly progression year after year. Broadly speaking, the longer you stuck at it, the better off you became. What's more, you could base your standard of living on this predictability – you could take on additional expenses in the almost certain knowledge that your ability to pay the bills was never going to come into question.

Not so with modern careers, however, where earnings can vary enormously from one year to the next and where occasionally it may be necessary to notch back your outgoings to enable you to exercise one of your choices. For example, you may decide to go freelance – in which case you will probably need to gear your finances to take account of a period at the start when there won't be much money coming in. Alternatively, you may decide that to advance your career in the direction you want it to go in you would be better off taking time out to get further qualifications.

It would obviously be helpful in these situations if some of your outgoings (your expenses) could be made to go up and down in line with your incomings. Though this won't be possible with every item of your domestic expenditure there is usually more scope than you think for introducing flexibility on these lines. For example, you could contribute more or less into a personal pension plan depending on how much you expect to earn in a given year. You could even decide to take a contributions holiday. Flexible mortgages are available too.

Key point

Getting your finances onto a more flexible footing will help you if the time should come when you need to make cut backs. More to the point, having to pay the bills won't be the reason why you can't exercise your choices.

Warning

Remember the point we made earlier in the book about not allowing yourself to become fenced in by expensive lifestyles? Mick is an example. He landed a top job with an overseas bank and on the basis of this he bought a large property and sent his two children to expensive private schools. Now Mick is finding that the job isn't to his liking (the people he works for are constantly making unreasonable demands). What Mick really wants to do is go back to the kind of work he did previously, but he can't do this because it would mean selling his house and disrupting his children's education.

Savings

Always do your best to put some money to one side so that you will have a war chest to dip into if, for example, you need to pay for a course or if you decide to go back to college full time. Getting into a savings habit is a good idea anyway. With the uncertainty of modern careers, it is always best to have something stashed away for rainy days.

Cultivating the right image

The word 'image' is a complete turn-off for a lot of people. They associate it with types such as image counsellors and style gurus and it is not surprising that the Joe and Jane Ordinaries of this world feel 'this isn't for them'. Image, however, has another and more serious connotation – a very important one as far as people who are managing their own careers are concerned. Indeed, acquiring a winning image is all part of adding value to yourself. Let's use this next case study to see why.

Case study 12: Diana, Penny and Rob

Diana is the newly appointed Chief Executive of a contract catering company – one of the leading names in the industry. Diana has been in her new position for just three months and already she can see a number of flaws in the management structure. Chief among these is the need for a really effective Operations Director – someone at the centre who will pull together the activities of the Regional Managers, co-ordinate resources and give the business a proper sense of direction.

Having got the board to approve the appointment of an Operations Director, Diana's thoughts next turn to suitable candidates. As far as internal contenders are concerned, she draws an immediate blank. No one in the organization has the right mix of experience and personal attributes. So she could advertise the job in trade journals and the local press, but this in her view gives her two problems:

- Anyone can reply to an ad in a newspaper and she could end up with a square peg in a round hole.
- Running advertisements, sifting through replies and carrying out interviews all take time and time is something she can't really afford.

It is concerns such as these that set Diana thinking about people she knows. Is there anyone among her past acquaintances who would make a good Operations Director?

The first person to cross Diana's mind is Penny. Penny and Diana worked for the same company for several years and they have kept in touch ever since. Penny is currently in a general management job with one of the smaller players in the industry. She is frustrated by what she sees as a lack of prospects for women managers in her company and Diana feels she would jump at the chance to join one of the big names. Penny is good at managing people and implementing new ways of working, but what bothers Diana about Penny is her habit of getting into bad personal relationships and the loss of focus on her job that usually ensues.

The other person Diana comes up with is Rob. Rob was briefly Diana's assistant in her old job, where he acquitted himself well in the short time that she knew him. Rob's biggest drawback is his lack of management experience. He is young and quick to learn but he has no track record to speak of in heading up large teams. On the plus side, Diana knows of no flaws in his character. He is consistent and always handles himself very professionally. He would probably make a very good Operations Director but there would be a learning curve for him to tackle first.

Given the choice between Penny and Rob, Diana rates them both very highly but she has to admit that Penny's greater experience puts her closest to the specification. What concerns Diana, though, is what would happen if Penny went through a bad patch in her personal life again. Would she put the job first or would she go on one of her downers, leaving Diana to pick up the pieces?

The latter, in Diana's view, is too great a risk to take so reluctantly she decides she must give Penny a miss. With Rob, on the other hand, what she clearly needs to do first is satisfy herself that he could handle the job of Operations Director. With this in mind she picks up the phone. She'll invite him to join her for lunch, she decides. Then after she's had a long chat with him she'll make up her mind.

The points to highlight from this case study are as follows:

• In sourcing suitable candidates for the position of Operations Director, how Diana is driven by two concerns. First is her need to feel comfortable about anyone she appoints. And second is her wish to avoid long, drawn out and resource consuming selection procedures.

• How these concerns cause her to turn to people she knows.

• How a flaw in Penny's character works against her. How Diana's knowledge of Penny puts her out of the running as far as being considered for the job is concerned.

• How Penny would have fared far better if she'd managed to keep her flaws to herself.

• Conversely, how Rob benefited from Diana's less detailed knowledge of him.

• How employers like Diana always play safe when it comes to making top appointments.

The lifelong interview

Though we don't yet know whether Rob is going to get the job, he is at least in with a chance – which is more than can be said for Penny. What the case study of Diana, Penny and Rob illustrates, though, is the importance of the image you put across as you go about your everyday business – the impression people you come into contact with form of you and how this can come back either to help you or haunt you as you move forward with your career.

A useful comparison to draw here is with going for an interview for a job you would really like to get. You dress smartly. You make sure you're on your best behaviour. You're careful about anything you say and, if there are any grey areas in your past history, you'll do your best to keep them under wraps. This contrasts with the rather less well-managed image you may put across to those who have dealings with you every day. Your appearance may not always be up to scratch. You are not so guarded in your conversations. You may even let your hair down occasionally and the odd less endearing aspect of your character may even slip out.

The problem here of course is that we're talking about projecting an image all the time, rather than during the 45–90 minutes that's the average for most job interviews. Harder? Yes it is – and this is what we mean by the **lifelong interview**. The consistency and application called for are not easy to achieve. It means, for example, that:

- you can't afford to have off-days
- you're never the first to dress down
- you don't get drawn into office gossip and tittle-tattle
- you don't denigrate your bosses and your colleagues behind their backs
- you don't blame others for your mistakes – if it's your fault own up to it
- you learn to keep your flaws to yourself
- you give some of the gloss you normally save up for interviews to every day.

Key point

The image you project is all important in leading others to take a positive view of your worth.

Headhunting

With Diana we saw an employer tapping into her own networks (people she knew from the past) to source suitable candidates for a job. In effect what she was doing was headhunting except, instead of enlisting the help of consultants, she was finding the people and making the approaches herself.

Professional headhunters (or executive search consultants, as they prefer to be known) also operate by tapping into their networks except, in their case, they make a living out of it. In fact, by buying a headhunter's services, you are paying for the privilege of accessing his/her networks and since headhunters are networkers *par excellence* it's a safe bet that their circle of contacts will be a lot wider than yours. What happens is this:

Example

ABC Cement Products' profits have slipped dramatically in the last two years and the board decides it's time to look for a new chief executive. DEF & Associates – a well-known firm of executive search consultants – is contacted and a specification is drawn up. Notably the new chief executive must be someone who has a proven track record in running a successful cement products business – possibly one of ABC's competitors. Armed with this specification DEF speak to their various contacts in the cement products world. Soon they have a list of names – people who have been recommended to them and who they now proceed to phone.

This example demonstrates that in order to be on the receiving end of a headhunter's approach:

- someone has got to know you; and
- what they know about you has got to be good.

Key point

Headhunters obtain business by reputation. Hence, with future billings at stake, they play ultra safe with any candidates they put forward. They seek people who are person-perfect and work-perfect. So, people with black marks on their record are automatically given a miss.

Notepad

The link between professional networking, projecting a successful image and getting your name onto headhunters' lists is one we will explore further in Chapter 8, Moving into the Future.

Using your added value to get a better deal for yourself

To sum up so far, we have seen how you can add to your value by:

- adding to your skills and qualifications; and
- working on your lifelong interview to acquire a better, more marketable image.

We will now look at how to use this added value to broker better deals for yourself; how to enhance your range of choices and open up your prospects as a consequence; how to ensure you arrive at the career destinations you have determined for yourself and not to get stuck half way. Again, let's start by using a case study – this time the tale of Julian.

Case study 13: Julian

Julian works in London for a well-known firm of management consultants who have offices worldwide. He specializes in financial reporting systems and, in his time with the firm, he has developed considerable expertise in this field. He is well-known to several of the firm's leading clients – many of whom ask for him by name.

Julian has heard on the grapevine that there is a vacancy for a project manager in the firm's New York office. This interests him for two reasons:

• The job would be a promotion giving him access to a higher salary and an attractive range of perks.
• New York is the firm's head office meaning that, if he worked there, he would be centre stage as far as any further promotion opportunities are concerned.

The first person to learn of Julian's interest in the job in New York is his boss, Dermot. Julian asks to see Dermot one night after work. During this meeting Dermot is largely non-committal. He likes Julian a lot and has a good opinion of him and his work but privately he doesn't want to lose Julian from the London team because his skills and experience would be difficult to replace.

Later that evening Dermot thinks through his options. He could, if he wanted to, block Julian's application, but he sees straight away that not letting Julian have a crack at the New York job would only serve to thwart him. The risk then would be Julian with a sore head touting himself round the industry where it wouldn't be long before someone snapped him up – just for his contacts alone. What's more, Dermot knows Julian is close to getting his MBA – which would make him an even more attractive prospect on the open market.

No, Dermot tells himself, losing Julian to New York wouldn't be good but having him working for the competition would be much worse. With this thought in mind he puts in a call to his opposite number in New York. He'll see first whether the rumours about the project manager vacancy are true, then, if they are, he'll put Julian's name forward.

Leverage

In Julian's case we have someone who has made a good job of adding value to himself:

- He has acquired expertise in his specialist field.
- He will soon have his MBA.
- He projects a good image.
- He has built up a useful network of contacts.

All of these factors combined exert **leverage** on his boss, Dermot. Dermot realizes that if he doesn't go along with Julian's plan then the consequences (in the shape of Julian working for someone else) could be nasty.

It is interesting to speculate at this point how Dermot would have reacted if Julian had not made such a good job of adding to his value – if, for example, his skills were of limited use or if the quality of his work was poor. Dermot would certainly not be pulling out all the stops, and as for the prospect of Julian going to work for someone else, Dermot would probably be rubbing his hands with glee. In short, leverage doesn't work where the estimation of your worth is low.

Key point

Adding to your value leads employers to form positive estimations of your worth, and this works to your advantage in the shape of the leverage that you can bring to bear when it comes to moving your plans forward. Notably, if their estimation of your worth is high they won't want to run the risk of losing you – meaning they'll be more inclined to go along with your ideas. This is what we call **silent bargaining power** and it is something that everyone who is in the business of running their own career should always be seeking to acquire. We will be looking more closely at silent bargaining power and its application in Chapter 7, Getting Results.

Asking yourself what pain you would inflict on your employer if you decided to leave is a good way of measuring your silent bargaining power. Would your skills be difficult to replace? Is there a lot of knowledge locked up inside your head? It is the answers to questions like these that will determine the success you're going to have when it comes to negotiating good deals for yourself.

Moving forwards and seeking continuous improvement

As a good manager of your own career, adding value to yourself is something you should always be striving to do. In other words you should see your development as a continuous and on-going process, one where:

• you are always aspiring to do something better; and
• you are constantly seeking to keep your skills and qualifications up to date.

This is not merely a way of avoiding stagnation, but also a way of ensuring that your silent bargaining power and your ability to exert leverage are not waning.

Keeping your development plan in focus

In turn, this means that your development plan isn't something you get out and dust down every once in a while when the mood takes you. Rather you should be in a constant dialogue with yourself on what you need in the way of further skills and qualifications to enable you to make your next step forward – and don't do what Darren did in our next short case study.

Case study 14: Darren

For a number of years Darren has worked as a Warehouse Manager for a distribution company and one of his ambitions is to get into sales. Darren, however, has never learned to drive and, though he realizes that a driving licence is essential as far as most sales job are concerned, the long hours of overtime he works plus his family commitments have always made it difficult for him to find the time to take lessons. He promises himself he will get round to it one day but, so far, he keeps putting it off.

The potential problem for Darren will be when an opportunity arises to get into sales – for example, when someone in his company decides to give him his big chance. The fact that he can't drive will then loom large as an obstacle and Darren could find the opportunity slipping away simply because his company can't afford to wait for him to learn to drive.

The moral to this tale? When opportunity knocks you must be ready for it. Conversely, don't squander your chances by making the mistake of putting your development plans on hold.

Notepad

We saw in Chapter 1 with the art of the possible how important it is to use 'what's there' and take advantage of opportunities that come your way. This connects with the point about being ready by having the right skills and qualifications in advance of the opportunities arising. The world won't wait for you and, as part of perfecting the art of the possible, it is important to remember this.

What about Darren? What should he be doing? The short answer is to look for ways and means of learning to drive. Could he, for example, make better use of his free time? Or does it mean putting aside some of his holidays for fitting in lessons? In most cases like Darren's the answer to the problem is to bring your development plan to the top of your list of priorities rather than make the mistake of putting it off to a more convenient time.

Questions and answers

Course only available during working hours

Q *I have ambitions to get into management and I want to do a course in employment law which involves attending full time for three days. I asked my firm for the time off but they said no for the reason that they could see no benefit to me in my present role as an administrative assistant. I looked into the possibility of doing the course in the evenings or at weekends but unfortunately it isn't available in the area where I live. Where do I go from here?*

A Book three days' holiday and do the course in your own time.

Taking on borrowings to fund the cost of going on a course

Q *Rather like Don in case study 11, I dropped out of university half way through my course and now I would like to go back to complete my degree because it would improve my job prospects. The problem I have, however, is that, thanks to a succession of poorly paid jobs, I'm flat broke – meaning there's no way I could meet the costs. A friend suggested I should take out a loan but I feel hesitant about doing this. What do you think?*

A   In principle there's nothing wrong with taking on short-term borrowings to fund the cost of going on a course. You're making an investment in yourself and this is the way to view it. What is perhaps more important for you, however, is to ask yourself whether doing the degree will really improve your job prospects as you seem to think. We say this because we come across a number of people in the middle years of their working lives who have taken themselves off to university and suffered great financial hardship only to find that doors don't magically open for them at the end of it. The result, understandably, is disappointment – and, in some cases, bitterness. What you must do, therefore, is take as many soundings as possible. For example, talk to a few recruitment consultants (employment agencies) and ask them if they think that having a degree would help you access the kind of career opportunities you are seeking. Alternatively, would your ambitions be better served by getting more work experience? Listen to the answers you get, i.e. don't shut your ears because the opinions expressed don't happen to fit in with your own ideas. Some people go back to university for kudos reasons. This is fine providing you realize what you're doing and that kudos doesn't pay off loans.

Blemishes on my track record

Q   *Frankly I've not made a very good job of my lifelong interview. I've held a succession of positions over the last two years, none of them for very long, and where, for one reason or another, the employer and I have usually ended up agreeing it would be better if we parted company. Is this a case of 'forget it' as far as any hope of adding value to myself is concerned?*

A   It's never too late to turn over a new leaf and you should start straight away. Ask yourself at the same time whether the string of failed jobs was your fault or whether you made bad choices. With the former, the answers are in your hands. With the latter, you clearly need to give more attention to targeting the right jobs – a subject we will look at in the next chapter.

Restraint clauses prevent me adding value to myself

Q *I work in sales in a very competitive industry where, yes, I could inflict considerable damage on my employer if I left and went to work for a competitor. The problem is, however, that my terms of employment have a restraint clause included in them which prevents me from joining anyone in the same line of business for two years. Where does this leave me in terms of my leverage?*

A The fact that you are on a restraint clause underlines just how sensitive your employer is to losing staff to competitors. What you must remember though is that your worth to your employer isn't just based on the harm you could do to it by picking off its customers. You probably have a lot of know-how locked inside your head which would be hard to replace; you know your way round the trade; you have contacts and so on. More to the point, if you do a good job and put over a good image, you will be seen as a valued employee – someone your employer will be at pains to keep. This could all add up to substantial leverage when it comes to seeing that your career aims are met.

Boss telling me I'm making a mistake

Q *I'm in a situation a bit like Julian in case study 13 where I want to work in one of our overseas offices – in my case Hong Kong. I put this to my boss and to my surprise, instead of saying she'd discuss my request with the Human Resources Manager, she told me I was making a big mistake. Pressed for a reason for this comment, she said the Hong Kong office was a backwater where people's careers get buried. For my part, I can't see the logic here. Two people who were recently made up to full partners both did time in Hong Kong and the firm actively encourages cross promotion of staff between offices. What should I do?*

A Check out where your boss is coming from. It could be that her real motive in discouraging you is to keep you in her team. Our advice? Stick to your agenda and, unless your boss can come up with a more credible reason for pouring cold water on your ideas, press the point that you want your request to go forward to Human Resources. If your boss is trying to hang on to you then it shows she has a high opinion of you, meaning, at some stage, the leverage should start to work. If it is just a case that she's pig-headed or disinclined for other reasons, you should start to pick up the signs from your further dialogues with her. (Chapter 7: Getting Results contains some ideas on going over the boss's head.)

Summary

No business will flourish unless you invest in it and the same applies to managing your own career. You need to determine what additional skills and qualifications you need to move you on the path from A to B. You then need to acquire those skills and qualifications by whatever means it takes and not to shirk from this task because otherwise you will be disadvantaging yourself in the pursuit of your objectives.

In this chapter we have looked at the business of adding value to yourself – making yourself a more sought-after commodity as far as the market for your talents is concerned. We have drawn your attention to the importance of the image you project as you go about your day-to-day work (your lifelong interview). The reputation you build up – not just for the quality of your work but also in terms of such factors as your character and reliability – plays a vital part in propelling you along your chosen path. It enables you to use professional networking effectively and, as we shall see later in the book, this has particular benefits for you as you seek to move onwards and upwards.

05
planning your moves

In this chapter you will learn:
- when it's right to explore your options
- targeting
- how to shop the market for your talents.

What's your next step? Having established the aim and put your personal development plan in place, how do you set about getting into forward motion? In this chapter we will look at:

- Taking stock of your situation – where you're at now and the choices that are open to you.
- Making moves versus staying put – factors weighing in your decision.
- Setting targets – the importance of not setting foot in the world without some clear idea of where you're going.
- Shopping the market for your talents intelligently – seeing what's 'out there' for you and applying selectivity.

Taking stock of your situation

First some revision. We saw in Chapter 2 how managing your own career starts with examining the choices you have and seeing how these choices tie up with your career aims. We saw also how choices can be extended with the application of a little imaginative thinking – how, for example, something that at first sight looks off beat and risky, such as working independently or making a complete change of career, can be brought within your range of choices. The idea in Chapter 2 was to get you to see that:

- there is always more than one way forward;
- part of the challenge of managing your own career is using the choices open to you intelligently;
- only by considering all of your choices will you be able to determine the full extent of the market for your talents.

Now let's look at putting some of this into practice. To help us do this we'll look at another case study – this time Andy.

Case study 15: Andy

Andy has worked for a small privately owned fencing contractor for a number of years, the last four of which have been spent as General Manager. Andy's boss, the proprietor, has always promised to give Andy a share in the business one day but, as the years have rolled by, nothing has ever materialized. Andy is now 44 and increasingly aware that he needs to get some firm commitment from his boss so, with this aim in mind, he brings the subject up one night after work.

At first, when reminded of his promises, the proprietor is evasive, saying that he needs to discuss the matter with his family first. Andy is puzzled by this remark. The idea of giving him a part share in the ownership was floated at the time he took on the General Manager's job – in other words he is surprised to learn that the proprietor hasn't mentioned it to his family previously. What's more, Andy hadn't bargained for the fact that the allocation of his share of the business was subject to a family consensus. He thought the proprietor had a free hand in the matter and that was certainly the impression that he gave.

Suspicious now that the proprietor may be trying to wriggle out of his promises and wondering what's at the back of it, Andy decides to make some discreet enquiries in the trade. One of the people he speaks to is the Commercial Manager of a major fencing manufacturer – someone whom Andy has known for many years and who has warned Andy previously that the proprietor is not trustworthy. From this source Andy hears a disturbing rumour. The business has been put up for sale, or so the story goes, partly to clear the proprietor's debts and partly to enable him to purchase a retirement home in Portugal.

Sadly for Andy this all has a ring of truth. The proprietor dabbled in an agricultural venture a few years ago in which he lost a lot of money. Also he has been to Portugal for six weeks recently, supposedly for a holiday though frankly Andy is now starting to wonder.

After talking the matter over with his wife, Andy decides to have it out with his boss. Again waiting for a suitable occasion one night after work, he confronts the proprietor with what he has been told. At first the proprietor is flustered, denying everything, but then, as Andy presses the point further, he confesses that he has put the business up for sale and that he has already received two enquiries. Flabbergasted, Andy asks why he could not be told what was going on – why the proprietor continued to string him along with the promise of a share in the business when he knew this would never happen. The proprietor says he had no choice in the matter. With creditors pressing, the bank told him to play his cards close to his chest.

Not sure whether to believe this or not, Andy talks to his wife again when he gets home later on. He tells her he is very critical of himself for being naïve and trusting the proprietor for all these years. More to the point he is concerned about the future. The new owners may not have a job for him and then where will he be? Out on his ear on the wrong side of 40 and with nothing except his redundancy money? Even worse, the fencing trade is all he knows and there's no other contractor of any note within a 50-mile radius.

Marrying your choices to your situation

Poor Andy – he has fallen into the trap of not having any agenda except for the one dangled in front of him by his duplicitous employer. He banked everything on a part ownership of the business coming his way and, when this proved to be an empty promise, he had no ideas of his own to fall back on. The result? Despair, embitterment and panic.

So what choices does Andy have now? To date, all he has considered is waiting in a cold sweat for the new owners to arrive and decide whether they want his services or not. In the event of them not requiring him his thoughts have progressed no further than the yawning chasm opening up under his feet and the prospect of having to find work in a different trade.

However, it is still early days as far as Andy is concerned and, once he has recovered from the shock of his boss's double dealing, he may be able to start to come up with some interesting ideas. However, let's see if we can help him.

Going back to your career aims

In Andy's case from what we know of him the aim he seems to cherish most is to run his own fencing business. After all, this was the carrot that his unscrupulous employer successfully dangled in front of him – presumably to keep him interested, motivated and 'on board'.

So the next question is, given the circumstance he's found himself in, is there any way Andy can advance his ambitions to have his own business? Are there any choices open to him that will move him in the right direction? Or is it all a lost cause as he seems to think?

What leverage do you have?

This is a useful place to start. What leverage does Andy have on his boss? What silent bargaining power can he bring to bear?

Here we're guessing but, as General Manager of the business with several years' standing, it seems safe to assume that Andy holds a lot of the keys. He's got contacts, we know, and his boss seems to be able to go off on long holidays without any serious effect on the business – all leading us to believe that Any deals with most of the day-to-day running himself.

So what would the fall-out be for his boss if Andy decided to leave? In terms of running the business it would probably give the proprietor no other option but to roll up his sleeves and do it himself. As someone with his sights set on retirement we can only imagine that the proprietor would not find this greatly to his liking.

There is an added dimension to Andy's leverage, however. What if he started up his own fencing company? What if he used his know-how and contacts to take away business? How would that affect the proprietor's plans to sell up? What would prospective buyers think if they found out that the ex-General Manager had just set up in competition down the road?

Because the proprietor is a shrewd character thoughts like these have probably passed through his head already and this could explain why he has tried so hard to keep Andy 'sweet'.

Exercising your choices

One choice open to Andy is to put in his own bid to buy the business. The leverage is there. The proprietor would be quick to appreciate the risks attached to turning Andy down. The leverage could also serve to reduce the asking price.

Of course, there are other considerations to buying a business – such as raising the necessary cash – but the points to note with Andy's case study are:

• how there are always choices (even in the direst situations); and
• how your value expressed in the form of leverage can be brought to bear.

Notepad

We will explore the use of leverage in pursuing career aims in greater detail in Chapter 7: Getting Results.

Making moves versus staying put

This is perhaps one of the hardest decisions you have to take. Whether to take your talents elsewhere or whether to play safe and stay where you are.

Positive risk management

We looked at risk in Chapter 3. Here we encouraged you to take a positive view of risk and not to let it be a reason for setting your feet in cement. Notably we encouraged you:

- to see the upsides as well as the downsides;
- to view the risk favourably if the upsides look good;
- conversely not to take risks where the upsides are inconsequential – for example moving jobs for a minor increase in salary;
- to take into account the risks of doing nothing – for example staying where you are and continuing to underachieve; and
- never to view anything as risk-free.

Returning to Andy, he probably has a number of choices open to him but, for the sake of this exercise, let's consider just three:

- staying put
- making a bid for the business
- going off and starting his own business.

Let's now consider the risks in each of these choices in turn:

- **Staying put.** One choice open to Andy is to carry on as normal, keep his head down and wait for the sale of the business to go through. The only obvious upside to exercising this choice is if he succeeds in keeping his job as General Manager – if the new owners decide to keep him on. The downsides, however, don't look too clever. The new owners could decide to bring in their own General Manager. Alternatively, Andy could find he likes his new bosses even less than his old one. Either way, the outcomes aren't good. As to Andy's ambition to have a stake in the ownership of the business, even if he survives the change of ownership, that's one he would have to consign to the back burner.
- **Making a bid for the business.** The upside here is that Andy realizes his ambition. The downside is he'll probably be in debt to the bank and paying off the interest on a loan – the nightmare scenario being if the business doesn't perform for any reason (e.g. a recession in the industry) and Andy gets into cashflow difficulties.

- **Starting his own business.** Here the upsides and downsides are much the same as with the previous choice except that, as a start-up, Andy will have rather more to contend with in terms of pressure on his cashflow. There will be however long it takes to build up the sales to a profitable level. There will also be his old firm under its new ownership fighting to get back any business he has taken away.

Set against this kind of positive risk assessment, of the choices open to Andy, putting in a bid for the business seems to be the one with most going for it. It is interesting to note that, viewed coldly at the outset, this did not appear to be the case.

Minimizing the downsides

A further advantage to carrying out a positive risk assessment along the lines we have suggested is that:

- the downsides are identified; and
- once identified, you can take steps to minimize them.

In Andy's case, for example, he could investigate changing the business from a sole proprietorship into a limited liability company.

Notepad

Andy's case study also illustrates how opportunities can present themselves quite suddenly and without any warning. This harks back to the art of the possible: always being ready for these situations when they arise; always being on your toes; never ever letting the moment of opportunity pass you by (it rarely comes back).

Advantages to pursuing career aims internally first

Andy's situation is possibly a little unusual in that choosing to stay put and doing nothing is pitted with downsides. For most people this won't be the case. Staying where they are will have little in the way of downsides apart from putting up with more of the same. The bigger downsides by far will be those attached to taking a step into the unknown – for example, changing jobs and then finding that for some reason it doesn't work out.

Where a lot of people go wrong with managing their own careers is to confine themselves *exclusively* to pursuing their ambitions externally, i.e. by making job moves. What they frequently overlook – or write off prematurely – is the opportunity to exercise a little leverage on their present employer and to cash in on some of the value they've added to themselves (a subject we will be returning to in Chapter 7).

> **Key point**
>
> Unless there are over-riding reasons for doing otherwise, always explore the internal route to realizing your ambitions first. Not only is there is less risk attached to it, there is the added advantage of having the leverage of your worth to the organization on your side.

Setting targets

Targeting is about being clear in your own mind where your ambition is taking you. It is particularly important when you set off on a shopping trip on the outside job market. The next case study demonstrates why.

> **Case study 16: Fay**
>
> Fay is a management accountant. For the last five years Fay has worked for a small company that provides a range of contract maintenance services to offices, banks and other commercial premises. Fay's problem is that because of the size of the company she lacks prospects. She enjoys her work and gets on well with her colleagues but she realizes that, if she is going to get any further up the ladder, she will have to make a move.
>
> Fay's first task is to revisit her CV. She prepared her CV when she applied for her present job and she is pleased that she thought to save it onto a disk. She is even more pleased to find that her CV doesn't require much in the way of alteration. Her current position needs to be added onto her employment history of course, and she has recently gained full membership of her professional association, but other than that her CV looks fine and ready for use.
>
> Over the next few weeks Fay makes a point of scanning the job ads in the local evening newspaper and in the various professional journals that she takes. She picks out any positions for which she

feels she is qualified and puts an application in the post. The result of this activity is that she gets invited to three interviews. Straight away, however, this gives her a problem because she has to make three separate excuses for having to have time off work. Even more awkward is when she has to ask for more time off to attend second interviews for two of the positions. The Managing Director gets quite prickly and reminds her that the half-year accounts are due for completion in a fortnight's time.

Fay is offered one of the positions. It is with a firm of travel agents who, after a bit of heart searching, finally agree to pay her the salary she is asking for. What concerns Fay though is that, in terms of promotion prospects, the job has no more to offer than her present position. The firm of travel agents is small and, though she will have the job title of Financial Manager, the responsibilities are really little different from her current ones. Fay realizes the right decision is to turn the offer down. What bothers her though is having to start her job search all over again. As to having any more time off for interviews, the Managing Director is already suspicious and sooner or later she knows he'll start asking questions.

This is an example of targeting going wrong. The result is time-wasting and Fay squandering her time on interviews that don't get her very far.

Key point

There is always a limit to the amount of time you can have off work without questions being asked and stock excuses like 'going to the dentist' can start to wear thin when they have been used a few times. As part of good career management you must always, therefore, view your time off work as precious and not to be frittered away.

Having your ideas thought out

The outside job market can be a hostile and confusing place, especially for those who are not familiar with it. Before setting out into it, therefore, it is important to have clear, thought-out ideas on what it is you're looking for. This is rather like going on a shopping trip – you get it done more quickly and more effectively if:

• you know what you want; and
• you know where you're going to find it.

In Fay's case, if she'd thought through her targeting properly she would not have applied for a job with employers who could offer her no more in the way of prospects than her present firm. Instead she would have confined her applications to, say, bigger organizations or organizations in growth.

Reasons for targeting

Targeting is about being selective. It has two purposes:

- it cuts down on time-wasting; and
- it cuts down on failure.

With Fay, the time she took off work to attend her interviews was already causing raised eyebrows to the extent that she was now feeling inhibited about making any further applications. What's more, her excursion into the job market had not yielded what she was looking for – inviting a feeling of dejection and discouragement.

Warning

Discouragement is something you need to avoid at all costs because it could lead to you giving up on your career aspirations for the reason that you feel the shutters are constantly being closed in your face. Failed job applications are a source of discouragement. Failed job applications can come in the shape of rejection letters or, as in Fay's case, jobs that don't measure up (poor reward for her effort). Proper targeting helps you to avoid discouragement because the directions you'll be setting off in will be the right ones.

Flexibility

In Chapter 1 we talked about the importance of:

- not having career aims that are cast in stone;
- being prepared to modify your ideas in the light of experience.

This also applies to targeting. Fay, for example, has learned from her job hunting experience that applying to firms that are little bigger than her own is largely pointless. She can gain from this experience by defining the target better next time.

Targeting and accessibility

It is also important that everyone else knows what your aims are: where you are coming from and what you are seeking to achieve.

Going back to Fay again, we saw that she spent some time tinkering with her CV. She brought her employment history up to date. She added on the fact that her membership of her professional association had recently been upgraded. What she did not do, however, was to include in her CV any mention of what she was hoping to achieve by moving jobs. The upshot of this is that any prospective employer reading Fay's CV wouldn't have any idea whether the job she was applying for lined up with her ambitions or whether it was a complete mismatch.

Key point

Employers are just as keen as you are that they don't put square pegs into round holes. Hence, if they know what it is you want out of life, they can help you form an appreciation of whether it's consistent with what they've got to offer. In Fay's case, if she had made it clear in her CV that she was looking for bigger and better prospects (nothing else) then it stood a chance that the firm of travel agents would have picked up the mismatch between her ambition and their job vacancy. For example, it could have been a point for discussion at a preliminary interview and all the subsequent time-wasting would have been avoided.

Your CV is an important vehicle for conveying this transparency and accessibility. There are other ways, however, of sharing your ambitions with the world and ensuring as far as you can that the directions you're setting off in are the right ones:

- Use face-to-face meetings such as job interviews to make your ambitions clear.

- If you are registered with an employment agency or a firm of recruitment consultants make sure they understand what kind of job opportunities you are looking for.
- Make your ambitions clear to people in your professional network – people who could be putting a good word in for you; people who need to be feeding out the right messages.

Shopping the market for your talents

Two thoughts for you to consider as you read this book are:

- There's a much bigger market out there for your talents than you think.
- There are big rewards for you if you can learn to shop the market intelligently.

Understanding the market

If you have read any of our earlier books you will be familiar with our division of the job market into its visible and invisible constituents.

- The **visible market** is the one that's there for you to see. It consists of jobs that are advertised – in newspapers, journals and on websites. You access it by keeping your eyes open.
- The **invisible market** is more difficult to perceive. It consists of jobs that aren't advertised and you can only access it by using *proactive sourcing methods* (read on).

Key point

People who are good at managing their own careers are people who are in touch with the full range of opportunities available to them. This means sourcing both the visible and invisible job markets.

Warning

Too many people confine their sourcing of opportunities to the visible or advertised market. In this way they only ever see a fraction of what's available to them and, as a result, they underachieve.

Reactive and proactive sourcing

This is simply terminology. **Reactive sourcing** is where the stimulus is provided by the employer, for example in the form of advertising. Here you are responding to an invitation to put yourself forward and the quality of your response is what counts. **Proactive sourcing** is aimed at the invisible market. It is where the stimulus comes from you.

Proactive sourcing techniques

Mastering proactive sourcing techniques is one of the keystones to successful career management. It includes:

- Putting your name forward by cold calling employers or sending them copies of your CV.
- Professional networking – letting it be known to your contacts that (a) you would be interested in hearing about opportunities and (b) what opportunities would interest you.
- Registering with firms of recruitment consultants – these are people who get to hear about opportunities before they are advertised.

Applying selectivity

You shouldn't put yourself forward for every opportunity you source, and this is the mistake that Fay made in case study 16. Instead, you apply *selectivity*. You review your targeting and pick out the opportunities that match your career aspirations and put to one side those that don't. In this way you will find that although you are chasing fewer and fewer opportunities, the opportunities are better targeted. You will, for example, only be applying for jobs that move you in the right direction and you won't be wasting your time on jobs that move you nowhere or in directions you don't want to go in.

Warning

There is no virtue at all in applying for hundreds of jobs in the hope that sooner or later one will come up trumps. All you succeed in doing is:

- chalking up 'sorry but no thank you letters' – a source of discouragement;
- squandering your precious time off work on a procession of pointless interviews.

Make your job applications count. Do this by targeting them properly.

Questions and answers

Is it wrong to trust your employer?

Q   *With reference to case study 15, was it wrong for Andy to trust his boss (the proprietor)? Is this what you are inferring and, if so, should everyone be more circumspect about promises that are made to them?*

A   Trust isn't the issue. Andy's mistake was having no agenda other than the one his boss set out for him (a part share in the business at some point in the future). What Andy really needed to do was set out his own agenda (to be the owner or part-owner of a fencing business within X years) then move from there to examining his choices. Waiting for his boss to deliver on his promises was one choice. Setting up his own business was another. Possibly a third was to go into business with a colleague or one of his contacts. The list could probably go on from there – the point being that Andy needn't have all his eggs in one basket. Admittedly, in his case, his boss wasn't trustworthy, but some other event could just as easily have got in the way of Andy getting his part share of the business – for example a cash crisis brought on by a period of unfavourable trading forcing the company into liquidation.

Targeting and the unemployed

Q   *I've been unemployed for two months and, though I take the point about applying selectivity to job applications, in my case I feel it's a luxury I can't afford. Any comment?*

A   Yes. The idea behind targeting is to get some structure into your search for the right opportunities and to stop you applying for 'anything and everything'. In your case, however, a far more urgent need has overtaken the need to be pursuing career aspirations – that is the need to see some money coming in to keep the wolf from the door. What to do? Get yourself fixed up with a job first and, as you rightly suggest, it would be silly to start applying rigid standards of selectivity. Take whatever is on offer, bearing in mind that something that uses your skills and experience will probably afford you better pay (targeting of a sort). You can turn your thoughts back to realizing career aspirations once you've got a regular source of income again. (The next chapter, When your Job is at Risk, deals with unemployment and the challenges it poses for people who are managing their own careers.)

Asking for interviews outside working hours

Q *I am in a similar position to Fay in case study 16. After receiving a measly pay increase at the end of last year, I applied for about 50 jobs and registered with a number of employment agencies. As a result, I was inundated with requests to attend interviews. At first I used up the few days' holiday I hadn't taken, but when that ran out I took the time off and phoned in with the excuse that I wasn't feeling very well. I notice recently that the boss's attitude towards me seems to have changed. For example she got quite shirty with me the other day when I asked to go on a course. What I realize I daren't do is take any more time off for interviews but, if anything, I'm even more desperate now to find something else. What can I do? What's crossed my mind is saying that I'm only available to attend interviews outside working hours.*

A You may find some employers are happy to see you out of hours but this is certainly something you shouldn't be banking on. What can you do? In the short term you must look after the job you've got and not do anything else that could put you on the wrong side of the boss. Following that, sort out your targeting. Applying for 50 jobs is ridiculous and we suspect from your apparent lack of success that these were not targeted in any proper sense of the word. As for your interviews, wait for things to calm down at work before you start asking for any more time off then, by applying selectivity, do your best to keep your interviews to a minimum.

No jobs match my target

Q *I'm doing as you suggest and being very selective about the jobs I apply for. The problem I'm having, however, is that very few jobs seem to match up to my target – so few that I am beginning to suspect that I am doing something wrong. What do you think?*

A It could be your targeting is working – in which case keep going. On the other hand it could be a symptom of:

• Targeting jobs that don't exist or that are only in scarce supply – go back to what we said about assessing the demand for your talents.
• Under-sourcing – typically failing to tap into the elusive invisible market and relying too much on jobs that are advertised.

Summary

One of the difficulties of managing your own career is that the number of choices facing you can be quite bewildering. Throw in the opportunities for working independently or doing a mish-mash of freelance, contract and/or assignment-based work and the bewilderment can turn into utter confusion!

In this chapter we have been looking at matching your choices to your career aspirations and seen how:

• The situation you're in has a great bearing on your exercise of career choices (the tale of Andy).

• Leverage is a key factor (the extent to which you can use your value to your employer to move you in directions that are consistent with your career aims).

• Because of leverage, seeking to realize your career aims internally is an avenue you should always explore first.

• Targeting is essential (having clear ideas on the direction you're going in).

• Targeting enables you to determine which opportunities to go for and which to leave alone.

• You need to ensure that you're viewing the full range of opportunities open to you.

• You will only do this by engaging both the visible and the invisible markets for your talents.

06

when your job is at risk

In this chapter you will learn:
- how to spot when danger lurks
- how to get the best out of losing your job
- unemployment and how to handle it.

We live in a world where little is certain and where calamity can and does occasionally overtake us. In this chapter we are going to look at:

- Knowing when your job is at risk: spotting the writing on the wall.
- Avoiding redundancy.
- The outsourcing option: turning bad news to your advantage.
- Negotiating severance terms and getting the best deal for yourself.
- Unemployment and the challenge it poses.

Knowing when your job is at risk

An important part of managing your own career is knowing when your job is at risk; that is, being able to recognize the signs that something's in the wind so you can click into emergency mode.

Case study 17: Gail

Gail is a training specialist. She works for a chain of retail stores and she spends most of her time visiting the various branches delivering training packages to groups of staff. Gail has been doing this job for the last four and a half years.

Gail's firm has been through a bad patch recently. Falling sales due to increased competition have already brought about the closure of two branches and there have been several redundancies among administrative staff at Head Office. A surprise development, however, is the arrival of a new Chief Executive – a man with a reputation in the retail trade for turning businesses round. This prompts Gail to talk to her boss Mike, the Human Resources Manager. One of Gail's concerns is the rumour she's heard that the new Chief Executive is a believer in reducing businesses to their basic functions – sales, logistics and finance – and anything outside these basic functions is either cut or outsourced to external suppliers. Mike nods and says he's heard the same rumours too. As to the reassurances Gail wants about her future, Mike says he's not in a position to give them. The best thing to do in his opinion is 'wait and see'.

The writing on the wall

'Wait and see' is all well and good, but what Gail clearly needs to do if her job is coming under threat is to get some options open. Too soon? It's never too soon when the writing's on the wall. It's a case of act now and don't procrastinate or you'll regret it later. Get some irons in the fire immediately.

Warning

Too many people ignore the warning signs and don't do anything until the redundancy notices have gone out. They lose precious time and time is always running against you when your job is at risk.

Signs that your job could be at risk

The arrival of a new chief executive is just one situation where heads could be about to roll. There are others too:

- Your organization isn't performing very well or isn't performing to the liking of people who count, e.g. the financial markets and/or large institutional shareholders.
- One of your large customers is in trouble or about to swap allegiances.
- Your organization is taken over or merged with another business (mergers and takeovers are usually accompanied by rationalizations and restructurings, meaning that jobs will disappear somewhere along the line).
- Your organization announces it is going to invest in new technology (new technology usually means fewer jobs).

Redundancy is, of course, not the only reason why your job could be at risk. Other situations also spell out danger:

- You get a new boss. Usually it works out fine but relationships are funny and no one really knows how the two of you are going to get on.
- You start getting warnings about some aspect of your job performance. Take special note if you don't see any reason why you're being singled out for warnings. There could be a hidden agenda and putting you through a disciplinary procedure could just be a convenient way of getting rid of you.

- Your attendance record is impaired by sickness or family problems. Small firms with a lot of commercial pressures on them find absenteeism particularly hard to cope with.
- The office politics start to turn against you. People in organizations tend to form camps that are locked in more or less constant rivalry – for example the sales and production camps found in many manufacturing companies. Great if your camp is in the ascendancy but if, for example, someone from the opposing camp is appointed to a key executive post it could be a case of 'watch out'.

In all of these situations it pays to start opening up some options as quickly as you can.

Avoiding redundancy

Sadly, modern employment conditions dictate that most of us will have to face up to redundancy at some point in our careers. Indeed some readers of this book will have had the bad luck to experience redundancy several times.

Ignoring the writing on the wall

Telling you to avoid redundancy sounds like a bad joke yet there are plenty of people who sleepwalk right into it. They see the writing on the wall and they do precisely nothing. They wait until the redundancy notices go out and even then in some cases they still do nothing. Why? Let's ask a few of them to explain their reasons:

> May: 'With seven years' service I was due a redundancy payment plus a special bonus. I would have lost the lot if I'd left before my notice expired.'
>
> Stanford: 'I figured on having a break between jobs. I planned to do some travelling then start making job applications when I got back.'
>
> Sian: 'I thought I'd leave applying for jobs until after I'd finished. That way I would be able to give it my full attention.'
>
> Mac: 'I wasn't worried about getting another job. I knew I could walk in anywhere and get exactly what I wanted.'

Dangers of not heeding the warning signs

May, Stanford, Sian and Mac are people who went on to spend several months out of work. Like everyone who has ever been unemployed for a long time, they found it a depressing and demoralizing experience. What's more, their finances were left in tatters and, in two cases, they ended up doing jobs that were way below their capabilities – just to get some money coming in.

What are the lessons here?

- Don't be dazzled by the cash. Redundancy payments and other handouts may look attractive but when viewed alongside the losses you sustain from long periods of unemployment, their attractiveness pales into insignificance.

- Unless the sums are massive, seeing redundancy and the cash that goes with it as an opportunity to pursue some long cherished personal ambition (e.g. travel the world) is a mistake. The time to start thinking about flying your kite is when you've got a steady income again.

- Getting another job always takes a lot longer than you think. Don't, therefore, put it off to a time when you feel it will be more convenient for you.

- The job market is a funny place and it pays not to make assumptions about it – for example, feeling you can walk into a new job straight away. Take particular note if the assumptions you are making are based on speculation rather than hard experience.

Key point

As a good manager of your own career always do your best to avoid redundancy by:

- seeing the writing on the wall;
- moving quickly and finding something else before the axe falls.

Notepad

One of the bigger disadvantages you face when you are out of work is feeling under pressure – the kind of pressure that leads to you:

- viewing employment opportunities that come your way in a better light than many of them deserve;

- as a consequence, increasing the chances of making a bad move (into a job that you would not have taken if the pressure had not been there).

We will be discussing this problem of pressure a little later in this chapter.

The outsourcing option

We looked at the outsourcing option in Chapter 3 and we saw in the case of Kuldip (case study 9) how, where the circumstances are right, you can turn bad news into good by offering to do your old job not as an employee but as an external service provider instead.

Bringing leverage to bear

If you want to follow the outsourcing route, one of the first questions you need to ask yourself is 'Is the idea sellable?'

The answer to this question is that a lot depends on the leverage you can bring to bear and, in Kuldip's case, the target for his leverage was his boss, Karen. We saw that Karen was driven by three factors:

- The previous good work done by Kuldip.
- The uncertainty of having to move to an (unknown) outside supplier.
- The nuisance to her if the outside supplier turned out to be useless.

In short, Kuldip was able to exercise some quite substantial leverage, meaning that the idea of outsourcing DTP to him was a very sellable one (as he found out). On the other hand it would not have been so sellable if, for example, his work record had been poor.

Notepad

In a lot of cases where outsourcing is identified as the way forward for providing services, the nitty-gritty of 'making it work' is left to middle managers like Karen. Interestingly, it is the Karens of this world who are also most susceptible to leverage. They are at the sharp end – when things go wrong, they're the ones to take the blame. Conversely, leverage doesn't tend to work on people at the top – people removed from the sharp end. This is why it would be difficult for Kuldip to conduct his negotiations directly with the new Chief Executive – if, for example, the Chief Executive had tied Karen's hands by appointing a firm of consultants to take over the DTP work. (There is a question at the end of this chapter which deals with this situation – see 'Outsourcing: where an external provider is already lined up'.)

Getting the best deal you can

Whether you would want to include the outsourcing option as one of your choices is a decision that's entirely for you. The point to introducing it here is that it can figure as a way of avoiding redundancy, though we appreciate that setting up as a freelance service provider won't be everyone's cup of tea. Let's say, however, that you do decide to go down this route and let's say that you manage to sell the idea to the Karen in your life. Then what? How else can you use your leverage to ensure you get the best possible deal for yourself?

As a freelance service provider you will need:

• equipment to do the job;
• an agreed basis for charging for your services.

The following would be useful to you here:

• Continued access to the equipment you used previously – or some arrangement for purchasing the equipment on preferential terms.
• A fee structure reflecting your former salary and taking into account the expenses that your work is likely to incur.

If you work out of an office you may want to negotiate continued use of the office or some financial arrangement to help you either set up an office at home or to rent somewhere.

As Kuldip found, your leverage will help you to secure these items on favourable terms. Bear in mind that 'making it work' will be as much in the interests of your ex-employer as it will be in yours.

Key point

Don't overlook the outsourcing option as an escape route from redundancy. It is very much 'flavour of the day' and many organizations are going down this path of replacing in-house functions with outside service providers. The beneficiaries in many cases are their ex-staff (people who were once on the list to be exited).

Notepad

Taking the outsourcing option is a way of setting up on your own without having the worry of getting through a start-up period. You have money coming in from day one and you're not put in the position of having to fight for business in a world where few people know you or the quality of your work. Take Kuldip as an example. He would be in for a long hard struggle setting up as an independent DTP service provider in competition with established firms. It could be several years before his profits matched up to his salary in his old job.

Negotiating severance terms

Let's say, however, that the worst comes to the worst and you're not successful in your attempt to avoid redundancy or your employment being brought to an end for some other reason. And let's say you tried your best but the various irons you put in the fire didn't work out for you. You now face the prospect of walking out with nothing to go to.

We now turn our attention to how you get the best possible deal you can – some cash in the bank to help you over the next few weeks/months or however long it is going to take you to get your career back on track.

Unless you happen to be in the fat cat league the chances of your employer providing a large golden handshake to take some of the pain out of losing your job is extremely remote. As the manager of your own career, you must therefore take the lead yourself in opening up discussion on severance terms. If you don't, and you leave the matter of how much you should be paid to your employer's largesse, you could be in for an unpleasant surprise. Let's again use a case study to pick up the points.

Case study 18: Roger

On the retirement of his boss, Roger was promoted to the position of Factory Manager. Before this, he spent five years as a Production Engineer. He was promoted on the basis of his technical ability. The company is involved in a specialized plastics forming process, and knowledge of machine settings and the intricate dies used in production was felt to be of paramount importance in appointing the Factory Manager's successor.

Roger had every confidence in his ability to do his new job. He had observed his predecessor at close quarters for the last five years. He had even spotted a number of areas where he felt he could do better.

Six months into the job, however, Roger found he was struggling. He was getting criticism from the Managing Director over a spate of machine breakdowns that resulted in late deliveries to customers. He needed extra maintenance personnel to deal with the breakdowns but the Managing Director wouldn't give him the authority to recruit. The upshot was that Roger was having to carry out some of the repairs himself and, since the factory worked around the clock, it meant he was putting in very long hours.

The crunch finally came when the Managing Director asked to see him one night after work. There was a general discussion about the state of the factory and then the Managing Director dropped the bombshell. It wasn't working out, he said, and it left him with no alternative other than to let Roger go. Two big customers had already given an ultimatum that they would take their work elsewhere if the problems in production weren't sorted out and two others were on the brink of doing the same. No, said the Managing Director, he needed a Factory Manager who could organize his resources effectively and clearly Roger wasn't the man for the job.

Roger could scarcely believe his ears. He reminded the Managing Director about his numerous requests for extra maintenance personnel. This, however, cut no ice. The Managing Director simply retorted that in his view what was needed was proper planned maintenance and better utilization of existing personnel. Roger had failed to do this hence the company needed to find someone who could.

Poor Roger. For all his efforts he still got the short, sharp exit treatment and his case study is a reminder that life in management can be tough and sometimes not very fair. So what is Roger left with? Unless a route back into his old job can be found for him, there is little else except to try to negotiate the best possible severance terms for himself. Since it sounds like his departure is imminent it's unlikely he'll be able to find another job to go to in the short time available. A period out of work therefore seems to be looming on the horizon and Roger has a mortgage to pay and a family to support.

What leverage do you have?

Talking about leverage to someone like Roger who has just been told that he is going to get the sack seems strange to say the least. After all, what possible leverage can he have? What fear can his leaving have when that's precisely what's planned for him anyway?

The answer is this:

- Deep down Roger's boss may be feeling bad about giving him the sack. It may be playing on his conscience.
- Dismissing Roger opens up the potential for litigation and no employer looks forward to the prospect of having to defend an unfair dismissal claim in front of an employment tribunal.
- Other senior managers won't be impressed by harsh treatment of one of their colleagues. It won't do much for the firm's image with its key people if Roger is seen to get a mean deal.
- Roger has probably got some useful knowledge locked up inside his head – knowledge that could do damage to the business if it found its way into the hands of competitors.

All these are compulsions on Roger's employer to come to amicable terms with him. In other words, this is his leverage.

What to ask for

You may be fortunate enough to have a clause in your contract of employment guaranteeing you a soft landing in the form of a big pay out if your career should go into a state of free fall (a so-called 'golden parachute'). Most of us, however, are not in this position. Apart from any notice due to us or any redundancy payments to which we are entitled, our exit terms are something we have to negotiate.

Given that you find your services are no longer required, what should you be asking for in the way of compensation?

- You are going to have to find another comparable job and that may not be easy if, like Roger, your knowledge and skills are specialized. How long is it going to take you to find one? Six weeks? Six months? A year? A guesstimate will serve to give you a basis for working out what you should be asking for as the monetary part of your compensation deal.

- Any new job you take will be a fresh start, meaning (a) you are more at risk and (b) you won't have service-related entitlements, e.g. the right to redundancy pay. Loss of service-related rights is therefore something you need to take into account when doing your calculations.

- You may have fringe benefits such as a company car or membership of a private healthcare scheme. Clearly you need to take these into account too (the cost of providing the same benefits paid for out of your own pocket). Alternatively your employer could agree to let you buy the car at a reduced price. Similarly, your employer could buy you into the private healthcare scheme for a forward period.

- If you are in an occupational pension scheme, you could find your entitlements suffer as the result of the termination of your employment. Ask a pension adviser to do the sums. Perhaps the company could enhance the transfer values made available to you or make a one-off contribution into a personal pension plan.

Key point

What we see developing here is the start point for your negotiation. Your employer will doubtless have different ideas on an appropriate figure of compensation. The aim is to reach an agreement.

Arriving at a settlement

You may find that your employer is prepared to make a compensatory payment to you on condition that you sign an agreement to say that you accept the money in full and final settlement of any claims you may have either now or at any point in the future. Here the advice is to seek guidance from a solicitor or other suitably qualified person – indeed your employer may be recommending that you do this. Where the sums of money are considerable, getting legal advice before you sign on the dotted line is a must.

Notepad

Any success you have in coming to agreeable terms on a financial settlement with an employer that has just sacked you is going to be determined largely by how much leverage you can bring to bear in the form of silent bargaining power. What this means in turn is that, where your silent bargaining power is downgraded for any reasons, your ability to reach favourable settlements is greatly impaired and, at worst, it could be a case of 'forget it'. (There is a question at the end of this chapter which deals with this point – see 'My employers won't give me anything'.)

Unemployment and the challenge it poses

But despite having done all you can to side-step unemployment, let's say the plan hasn't worked and you now find yourself without a job to go to. As a good manager of your own career what do you do next? Let's take a look at another case study.

Case study 19: Everton

Everton is an economist with a background in sales and marketing. For five years Everton worked as a business analyst for a large retail group identifying and reporting on consumer spending trends. A change in top management, however, resulted in the team to which he was attached being disbanded and Everton being made redundant.

At first Everton wasn't too dismayed about losing his job. He received a generous pay off in the shape of three months' salary on top of his redundancy entitlements, hence he didn't feel under any great pressure to start looking for another position straight away. In fact he and his girlfriend went off on a holiday for three weeks as soon as he finished, figuring there'd be plenty of time for sending off applications when he got back.

Everton set his sights on finding another job as a business analyst. After all, it was a field of work in which he had considerable experience and where he felt he would have little difficulty in selling his skills to prospective employers. He also felt it was reasonable to be asking for the same kind of salary that he was earning in his last job. As to relocation this didn't interest him because he and his girlfriend had recently taken out a mortgage on a flat.

Everton therefore decided on a four-pronged approach:

- First, he sent his CV to five large retail organizations based within commuting distance of where he lived enquiring if they had any vacancies for business analysts.
- Second, he made a regular point of scanning the job ads in the local evening paper.
- Third, he registered with three firms of recruitment consultants in town who specialized in sales and marketing appointments.
- Fourth, he registered online with two well-known firms of internet-based consultants.

After three weeks the results of Everton's efforts on the job scene were as follows:

- Only two of the five retail organizations replied – one to say they had nothing for him currently but that they'd keep his CV on file; the other to inform him that they had a vacancy on their customer care team and a number to ring if he was interested (Everton wasn't).
- No ads for business analysts appeared in the local evening paper although Everton noticed that there were always plenty of vacancies for people in sales and marketing (jobs he knew he could do but jobs that were way below his capability – jobs that probably paid poor salaries).
- The three firms of recruitment consultants came up with nothing.
- The Internet-based consultants e-mailed him details of several vacancies but in all cases they were either in other parts of the country or totally outside his field.

Slightly puzzled by his lack of success, Everton decided nevertheless to keep going. He sent his CV to some more retail organizations. He continued to keep his eyes on the ads in the paper. He registered with a few more firms of consultants.

Let's pause there for a moment to take stock on what has happened to Everton so far:

- After a lackadaisical start he did quite well and got a number of irons in the fire.
- He targeted – another job as a business analyst on a similar salary to the one he earned previously and within the same area.
- He attacked both the visible and invisible markets – the latter by mailshotting his CV to selected employers and by registering with various firms of consultants.
- He applied selectivity to the jobs he sourced. He didn't apply for the job in customer care. Similarly, he didn't apply for the sales and marketing positions he saw advertised in the paper or the vacancies notified to him by the internet-based consultants. He viewed all of these as 'outside his target'.

Now let's go back to the story.

Case study 19: *continued*

After two months out of work Everton began to feel the first twinges of anxiety. With the expense of the holiday and furnishing the new flat his funds were starting to run short. The benefits he received plus the money his girlfriend earned as a clerical assistant didn't add up to much compared with the bills that kept coming in. As for the job hunting, he still continued to have no joy. Two more organizations replied to his mailshot but only to say again that they had no suitable vacancies. He spotted one job in the paper that seemed like a possibility and sent in an application (he was still waiting to hear back).

The consultants likewise continued to come up with nothing and, failing to understand why, Everton decided to pay one of them a visit. Here he spoke to a senior consultant who confirmed that they had not been able to find anything suitable for him and blamed the general state of the market. Everton explained that he was becoming desperate and asked if anything could be done for him. The consultant said she noticed he'd had previous experience in sales and, if he was prepared to consider jobs in sales, then that would open up a wider range of possibilities for him. Everton said he wasn't too sure. He enjoyed his work as a business analyst and found it challenging. Taking a job in sales, on the other hand, seemed like taking a backward step.

Another month went by and Everton and his girlfriend found they were starting to feel the pinch. They had cut down drastically on their lifestyle but they were still finding it hard to make ends meet. Worse still, Christmas was coming soon and they had no idea how they were going to be able to afford the expense. The job Everton applied for came to nothing. The company wrote back saying that it had decided to shelve the vacancy (but they would review the situation again in the New Year). The final straw came when the car broke down and Everton got an estimate from a garage on how much it was going to cost to put it back on the road. No, they decided, Everton was going to have to find something even if it meant taking a job in commission-only sales. He'd ring the consultants next day and tell them to cut the frills.

Chasing targets that are too narrow

What we are seeing with Everton is someone chasing a target that is very narrow (a job as a business analyst in a certain locality and at a certain salary). The fact the target is narrow is evidenced by the lack of success that his reactive and proactive sourcing has brought. In short, he has searched the market for his talents and found that:

- opportunities for suitably recompensed business analysts are thin on the ground in the town where he lives;
- the opportunities only come up from time to time.

In more normal circumstances what Everton would do is to keep going and wait for the right opportunities to come up. Either that or go back to his targeting and – in the light of the feedback he has received from the market – adjust his target in some way – for example, introduce a broader range of jobs into his specification.

The problem for Everton, however, is that tweaking targeting benchmarks in the light of experience takes time and this is something he doesn't have. Because he is out of work financial pressures are building up and the demoralizing effect of not having any success has had a further undermining effect. The result for people like him? Triggered often by an event (e.g. a big bill) their whole approach falls apart and they end up taking whatever happens to be going. Needless to say this is usually something way below their capabilities and, as a consequence, what follows is not very good.

Multiple targeting

So what's the lesson here? Simply this: when you are unemployed time isn't on your side and pursuing narrowly defined targets is a luxury you can't afford. What you must do instead is as follows:

* At the outset try to avoid entering into any preconceived opinions about the market for your talents. In particular, don't see getting another job as a walkover. If you do find employers are queuing up for you, great, but if you don't you could be in for a big disappointment and disappointments of this kind can be the seeds of discouragement.
* Look at the *range* of your talents, and then try to identify not just one target but several. Using Everton as an example, what else would his experience lend itself to? For instance, could he look at a job where analyzing business trends is combined with a broader sales and marketing role?
* Continue to apply selectivity but apply it to a number of targets – not just one.
* Use all the sourcing options open to you – proactive and reactive. In Everton's case, he did quite well with his sourcing except he omitted to try tapping into his professional networks i.e. his contacts in business. More unemployed people find work through professional networking than by any other method and it is important to remember this.

By proceeding in this way you will be giving yourself the best chance possible that:

* your period out of work won't last long and will come to an end well before financial pressures and discouragement start to bear down on you;
* because your approach is targeted, the job you get will be a reasonable one.

Questions and answers

Big pay off if I stick it out to the end

Q *My company is in the process of transferring its production to the Far East and, along with three hundred others, I am due to be made redundant in three months' time. One of the problems the company faces is that, in order to maintain the continuity of supply to its customers, production must carry on right up to the date of the transfer and this means retaining key people like me right to the bitter end. To this effect the company have promised us a big bonus if we stick it out and don't leave before our redundancy date – but, taking your point about getting some irons in the fire as quickly as possible, won't it put some employers off when they find I'm not available for another three months? In other words won't it be best to postpone my job seeking until a little nearer to when I finish?*

A   Three months sounds like a long time to find another job but with putting out feelers, making applications, attending interviews and second interviews, it's amazing how quickly the weeks go by. So no, don't postpone your job seeking because you will probably find that a sizeable chunk of the three months has already ticked away by the time you are offered a job, so the dilemma over whether to forfeit your bonus or not probably won't arise. If it does then we would advise you to be frank with prospective employers about your predicament. Some will be prepared to hold the job open for what remains of the three months whereas others won't. With the latter group make sure you do your sums before you turn the job down. What does this bonus mean in real terms? Will it compensate you for, say, having to spend three months on the dole? Will it compensate for your loss of earnings if you have to take a stop gap job for a period to keep the wolf from the door?

Outsourcing: where an external provider is already lined up

Q   *I work as a pensions manager for a large company and a few weeks ago I was told that, with effect from next year, the company will go over to using a firm of outside pensions advisers – meaning I and my two staff will be made redundant. Seeing that the decision to go to an outside provider is a 'fait accompli' are there any options in this for me?*

A   Two that we can think of:

- First – and providing you're happy to go down this route – there's still no harm in putting yourself forward as an outside provider i.e. submit a competitive tender. Who knows, with leverage on your side you may be able to persuade your company that you're a better bet than the people they've got lined up.

- Second, perhaps you could get a job with the outside advisers. Bearing in mind you have no direct leverage on these people other than your skills and experience, the best way to go about exploring this option is through your company. As a big future client they have quite substantial leverage on the outside adviser and this could be made to work in your favour.

Unfair dismissal claim will ruin my lifelong interview

Q *I can't think of anything more likely to alienate my ex-employer than bringing an unfair dismissal claim against them. How can this possibly square with what you had to say about the lifelong interview?*

A The point about litigation arose when we looked at the leverage you had when it comes to negotiating severance terms. The threat of litigation formed a part of this leverage because employers find the prospect of going before an employment tribunal very daunting. The threat, however, is one that is in the employer's mind rather than in any words that pass your lips, i.e. it is an implied rather than explicit threat – hence the term *silent* bargaining power. As to bringing an unfair dismissal claim against an ex-employer, our own view of this is that, for the reasons you suggest, it should always be seen as an action of last resort and reserved perhaps for occasions where an employer has caused considerable detriment to you.

My employers won't give me anything

Q *I didn't really put a lot of effort into my last job and, after a series of warnings, I finally got the sack. Frankly, I can't see my employers coming up with a severance deal for me, can you?*

A Frankly no. More to the point, what your question underlines is the all-important link between your lifelong interview and the leverage you can exert in the form of silent bargaining power. Sorry to put it like this but if your worth to your employer is zero to minus, then they won't feel inclined to dig into their pockets.

Summary

Life doesn't always go smoothly and, as part of managing your own career, you also need to be able to manage your way through periods of adversity. Sadly, there is an increasing lack of sentiment about people in the world of work today and we are constantly reminded of the extent to which we are at the mercy of the corporate whim and the state of the balance sheet.

In this chapter we have looked at:

- How important it is to spot when the writing is on the wall and to take action immediately.
- How it is best to avoid the axe by getting out before it falls.
- In some circumstances how bad news can be turned to your advantage by exercising the outsourcing option.
- How you still have leverage and how it can be used to negotiate severance terms.
- How looking for a job when you're unemployed is very different and how multiple targeting can help you shorten the period of time you spend out of work.

The message is that every career has its ups and downs. You need to learn how to manage both.

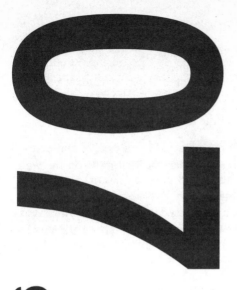

07

getting results

In this chapter you will learn:
- how to exercise bargaining power
- how to put forward a case
- how to judge which opportunities are for you.

Taking the management of your career into your own hands also means taking responsibility for ensuring it advances in the direction you want it to take, and not on some other path determined by someone else (someone who may not have your best interests at heart; or someone whose judgement you may not trust). In this chapter we will look at the business of achieving aims in the context of a self-managed career. We will cover the following:

- Understanding bargaining power – the leverage you have on employers when it comes to realizing your aims.
- Communicating your ideas and putting forward a case.
- Monitoring your progress.
- Using your networks in organizations to advance your aims.
- Evaluating opportunities and putting the art of the possible into practice.

Understanding bargaining power

We have already touched on the subject of bargaining power a number of times in this book, but now let's try and pull a few of the lessons together because it's important that you fully understand the nature of bargaining power before you put it to use.

Constituents of bargaining power

As we've seen in earlier chapters, bargaining power roughly equates to your worth to your employer and it has a number of constituent elements:

- **Your job performance.** Your worth to your employer will obviously be greater if you are good at what you do.
- **Your image.** Your worth will be enhanced if you project a good image. On the other hand, if you are seen as lazy or a trouble-maker, your worth will be devalued (the lesson of the lifelong interview).
- **Your skills.** If you have a good up-to-date range of skills your employer will place a higher value on you than if you do not. If some of your skills come under the heading of *scarce* skills then this will enhance your worth even further.
- **Your knowledge.** If you have access to know-how – if, for example, you're the person your colleagues turn to when they're stumped – then this will also add greatly to your worth.

- **Your contacts.** If you know people in your business or profession then this will likewise add to your worth. Contacts, of course, figure highly in rating the worth of people who work in sales.

Notepad

Remember how we saw in Chapter 4 that worth or value is not some static quantity but something that you can add to? Similarly you can subtract from your value by, for example, letting your skills lapse or relaxing your effort.

The leaver test

This, you remember, is a handy way of measuring your bargaining strength. How would your bosses react if you handed in your notice? Would they be rubbing their hands with glee? Or would they be thrown into a spin because your talents would be sorely missed and difficult to replace?

Notepad

The leaver test is useful because at the back of your bosses' minds when responding to any career aspiration you put forward is what would happen if you decided to pack your bags and take your talents elsewhere. Admittedly, if they would be glad to see you leave, then how they responded would hardly matter. But if they put a high price on your head, then they would be very aware of the risks of being unresponsive to you.

Silent bargaining power

The main point to understand about bargaining power is that it is very subtle and doesn't need spelling out because everyone knows the score. Therefore, you don't need to remind your bosses that your talents are transportable every time you seek to realize a career ambition. They will be perfectly aware of the consequences of saying no to you and won't need any reminding. On the contrary, reminding them could be seen as making a threat and, as we shall be seeing shortly, threats have a habit of inviting negative responses. In short, they can be counterproductive.

As we noted earlier, the *implied* rather than *explicit* nature of the force you are releasing when you enter into discussions with your employer is the reason we refer to it as *silent* bargaining power. It is what you use to exert leverage on your employer – leverage that will encourage your employer to respond favourably to your ideas rather than go against you or do nothing.

Key point

Amassing silent bargaining power is what all effective managers of their own careers seek to do. With silent bargaining power on their side they can move their career aspirations towards more favourable outcomes.

Communicating your ideas

What is quite certain is that you won't get very far with your ambitions if you keep them to yourself. Obvious? Perhaps, but surprisingly a lot of people go wrong with communicating their ideas as the next case study illustrates.

Case study 20: Laura

Laura works as a sales team leader for a firm of steel stockholders with service centres throughout the country. She has been doing this job for the past five years and feels it's high time her efforts were rewarded by being given her own service centre to run. However, she has now been overlooked three times for promotion and she is starting to lose hope.

So what's going on here? Why has Laura's career ground into gridlock? Is it something that she's done wrong?

On the contrary, the real Laura behind this case study had an almost exemplary work record and was thought of very highly by her seniors. So why was it then that she was not picked out for promotion? Why were the opportunities offered to others and not to her? We put these questions to her boss and his reaction was one of total surprise. He had no idea, he said, that Laura was interested in managing a service centre. He'd always assumed that she wanted to remain in sales – after all, she'd never said anything to lead him to believe otherwise.

Making your aims known

The underlying issue to Laura's case is: whose responsibility was it to open up the dialogue about her future? Was it Laura's? Or was it her boss who should have been 'saying something'?

Sadly, there are a lot of people like Laura – people who have been overlooked because their aims have been misread. But why does this happen? Most of us feel some reticence when it comes to opening up on a subject like our ambitions. On the whole we would probably prefer it if someone else (for example, our bosses) broached the subject. When they don't we tend to say nothing – hoping that an occasion will present itself at some point in the future or that, somehow or other, the message will eventually sink in. Part of the problem here, of course, is that putting forward our career aims can start to seem pushy and most of us don't feel comfortable with this. The result? We stay silent and we find ourselves in similar situations to that of Laura.

Waiting for your employer to initiate discussions on the next step in life is what happened in the traditional paternalistic model of career management. Your bosses did the thinking for you and then provided you with the wherewithal in the shape of suitable opportunities. But this is not the case today, of course. If you wait for your bosses you could end up waiting forever or, like Laura, you will take the view that there's no hope for you. The probable result? You will take your ambitions onto the outside job market and try your luck there.

> **Key point**
>
> Take responsibility for communicating your ideas. Don't assume your bosses understand your ambitions because, nine times out of ten, they don't.

Exploring the internal route first

Earlier, in the context of risk management, we advised you always first to explore the internal route to realizing your ambitions. A further reason for giving you this advice is so that you can get your silent bargaining power working for you. Your worth to your employer will serve to exert leverage of the kind that you could never bring to bear on an outside employer.

Notepad

A point to note in passing is that this extra leverage will help you to realize career aims that are intrinsically difficult – for example, making a big leap up the ladder, negotiating more favourable contractual terms or effecting a complete change of career. Needless to say, where you have little or nothing in the way of leverage, aims such as these will be hard to attain. Therefore, the message is that if you are trying to achieve something that is either highly ambitious or slightly offbeat, see what joy you have with your own employer first – i.e. before you jump into the relatively hostile world of the outside job market.

Let's now look at the task you face. You are going to communicate your ideas to a boss who may be about to hear them for the first time. What do you need to consider?

Timing your approach

First, you need to pick the right moment for having a discussion. Where a formal appraisal system is in place, an appraisal interview may present you with such an opportunity. On the other hand, if what you are seeking is pressing and the next round of appraisal interviews aren't for another nine months, then you may have to move on to Plan B.

What is important about the timing of the meeting to discuss your career aims is that:

• it takes place at a time when interruptions are least likely – for example, after hours;
• it won't be cut short by other engagements – for example, your boss has another meeting to go to.

To an extent, the timing of the meeting will be in your boss's hands but you should seek to pre-empt the difficulties outlined above by making it clear that:

• you want to talk about your future;
• you need at least half an hour.

Suggest a meeting after regular office hours and leave it to your boss to agree.

The aims of the discussion

This is quite simple. The aims are:

- to communicate your ideas; and
- to listen to the reaction and pick up any feedback.

Staying positive

Staying positive is very important. Anything you say has to be said within a positive framework – for example: 'I like it here, I would like to make my future with this organization and this is the way I see my career developing.' Conversely, anything that has negative overtones won't serve to further your interests because it automatically invites negative responses. The following are examples of negative statements:

- Any accusation – for example: 'You said you'd look at my salary at the end of the year but you never did anything about it.' A statement like this automatically puts the person to whom it is directed onto the defensive. The result? You will have an uphill struggle to get the conversation back onto a constructive track.

- Anything that conveys an impression of conflict – i.e. you versus the company. Often this can be avoided by the right choice of words. A good tip here is to stick to the first person plural when talking about the company. For example, 'We said we'd look at my salary last year' sounds much better than 'you said' or 'they said'.

- Moans and groans – particularly anything that is ancient history and has no bearing on your present situation. Even if the company did treat you shabbily in the past, raising it now could give the impression that you are walking round with a chip on your shoulder. Needless to say, this will do your image no good at all.

- Any statement that doesn't offer a solution – for example, 'I'm not happy with the way my career is progressing' provides nothing in the way of a solution and can be perceived as whinging, if you're not very careful. It is much better if you can qualify a remark like this by adding what you would see as the solution to your problem – for example, promotion to a team leader's position within the next 12 months.

Warning

When communicating your aims to your boss it's often hard to resist saying what you would do if your aims are not met. For example, Thomas said he wouldn't take any more work home unless the company could come to a more favourable arrangement for paying him, while Stephanie told her boss that she would hand in her notice if she didn't get the pay rise she wanted. What both of these people sought to do was bring their bargaining power to bear in a more overt or explicit way by making threats.

Is there anything wrong with this? The answer is yes. Threats invite defensive postures, meaning that the main item on the agenda (i.e. your career aims) gets pushed into second place. What's more, organizations don't always respond to threats in the way that you hope. In Thomas's case he got a sharp reminder that the work he was doing at home was part of his terms of employment and, if he refused to do it, he would get the sack. As for Stephanie, her boss told her that he didn't like the idea of being blackmailed, so, as far as her pay rise was concerned, she could go and whistle. This then placed her in a difficult position – either she had to find another job or lose her credibility. Poor Stephanie – she didn't really want to leave but, if she stayed, she realized that any silent bargaining power she may have had was gone. The message? Don't make threats unless:

• you've thought through the ramifications; and
• you're prepared to carry them out.

Notepad

There is a question at the end of this chapter that deals with explicit bargaining power and the use of threats: see 'What's wrong with blackmail?'

Delivering the message

The point to silent bargaining power is that the need to make threats doesn't arise. Your boss will be fully aware of the consequences of stone-walling you, hence there should be no need to spell it out. So, returning now to the aims of your meeting with your boss, you need to consider the following:

- Your boss needs to understand you and the best way to achieve this is by keeping your remarks as brief as possible. Say what you want to say, listen to what your boss has to say in response and then, as far as you are concerned, the meeting is over.

- Avoid getting drawn into arguments. If your boss is hostile to your ideas leave it at that. It probably means you are one step closer to finding out that your aims aren't realizable – or it could simply mean that your boss is having a bad day. (You know the character. You know the signs.)

- If your boss is non-committal or says something along the lines of 'I'd like to think over what you've said', then read this as coded language for meaning that you are asking for something that is outside your boss's remit and he/she needs to consult with someone higher up the ladder.

- If your boss says that he/she needs to speak to someone higher up, see if you can get some measure of how sympathetic he/she is to your ideas, i.e. how much effort is likely to go into arguing your case.

- If your boss comes up with constructive suggestions such as you need more experience, listen carefully to what he/she has to say.

By the end of the meeting you should have achieved your original two aims, namely:

- you've delivered the message; and
- you've listened to the feedback.

Your silent bargaining power will now be working for you and all you have to do is sit back and wait.

Monitoring your progress

Having communicated your ideas correctly, what you want to see soon is some evidence that you are making progress, i.e. that the message has sunk home and that someone, somewhere is paving the way forward for you. But what if nothing happens? What if the boss doesn't raise the subject with you again or seems to have forgotten? Let's use the next case study to explore some of the difficulties people face when trying to progress their career aims.

Case study 21: Marie

Marie has been the Financial Manager of her company for the past seven years. She is now 38 and keen to be given a seat on the Board of Directors – a promotion she feels she richly deserves. Her predecessor was on the Board of Directors and she can see no reason why the same privilege should not be extended to her. What's more if her company is not going to promote her she would rather know soon so that she can make alternative career plans while she's still on the right side of 40.

With these thoughts in mind, Marie asks to see the Managing Director one night after work. At this meeting she spells out to him the direction she would like to see her career moving in – i.e. a seat on the Board in the not too distant future.

The Managing Director is cordial as always and listens attentively to everything she has to say. His facial expressions, however, give away nothing and when she's finished speaking, he simply says that, since Board appointments are matters for the Board and not for him acting on his own, he will have to refer the subject to his colleagues. Marie tries pressing him by asking him how he would view her appointment. The Managing Director, however, side-steps her question by repeating that any opinion would need to be the opinion of the Board and not of any one individual.

Though the Managing Director is starchy and stand-offish by nature, Marie is still a little disappointed by what she sees as his unhelpful response. What should she read into it? She has no idea. She supposes it will be a case of 'wait and see'.

Six months go by and although Marie has many conversations with the Managing Director on a whole range of other topics, he makes no mention of her appointment to the Board or whether he has discussed the subject with his colleagues. So, steeling herself one afternoon, Marie decides to ask him point blank if there is any progress to report. The Managing Director seems at once uneasy and slightly flustered. He talks in general terms for a few minutes then says that, yes, he did raise the subject with his colleagues at the last Board meeting but, because there was a full agenda, it was one of a number of items that had to be carried forward to the next meeting in three months' time.

Marie reflects on this later in the day. The more she thinks about it, however, the more she feels convinced that the Managing Director is not being straight with her. As to why, she has no idea.

So what is going on behind the scenes in Marie's company? Is the Managing Director telling the truth? Or is he buying time for some reason best known to himself? Or has Marie already been given the thumbs down and the Managing Director is simply putting off telling her? Is he hoping the subject will just 'go away'?

Putting a time limit on the realization of your ambitions

Whatever the reasons for the Managing Director finding it hard to give Marie a straight answer, she is right to be concerned that there is no progress to show with the realization of her aim. It means:

- Either: the aim isn't realizable for some reason – for example, the Board won't open its doors to women.
- Or: Marie's silent bargaining power isn't working.

Agonizing too much over whether it's the former or the latter is to some extent irrelevant. All that matters is that, if Marie continues with her bid to be put on the Board, she could be falling into the trap of banging her head on a brick wall. Since this will achieve nothing other than inflicting pain, it's an activity she should disengage from as soon as the signs are there.

What this means in practice is:

- Don't drive yourself mad trying to force employers along roads they don't want to go down.
- Instead, manage the situation and set a time limit on how long you are going to give your employer to come up with what you're asking for.

In Marie's case a reasonable test of her silent bargaining power would seem to be to wait for the outcome of the next Board Meeting and to view any further prevarication as an indicator that nothing's going to happen for her (or that it won't happen for a long time). The signal then would be to start running through her options and getting some irons in the fire. Her company could still come up trumps but at least she won't be in the position of relying on them solely for the realization of her career ambitions.

Warning

There are many people like Marie who spend precious years of their lives hanging round waiting for employers to come up with the right opportunities for them and then find that they don't. The lesson here is not to squander your time and effort on employers who are never going to deliver. Instead, be very strict with yourself on how long you are going to give them. Don't let those precious years slip away because they won't come round again.

Using your networks to advance your aims

Networking is a subject all on its own and one that we shall be touching on again in the final chapter. Suffice it to say at this stage that developing effective networks is an important part of managing your own career and a powerful tool when it comes to advancing your aims.

Developing networks

A mistaken view of professional networking is that it consists of pressing your credentials on an ever-increasing number of people. This is not the case. Professional networks are entirely organic and should be seen as such: a natural consequence of being in a career and requiring no artificial growth stimulants of any kind.

Professional networks tend to consist of a mix of people, typically:

• People you meet in education – for example, at university or at business school.
• Work colleagues past and present: people you work with currently; people who have moved on and who now work elsewhere.
• Business contacts such as customers and suppliers – or people working for competitors that you meet through bodies such as trade associations.
• Professional contacts, i.e. people in the same line of work as you that you meet, for example, through professional bodies or because you belong to some special interest group.

> **Notepad**
>
> An important point to note is that any network needs a thread of common interest or shared experience. In the case of a professional network, the common interest or shared experience is provided by your work.

Internal and external networks

Some of the people you network with will be in the same organization as you whereas some of them won't. This means your network has internal and external dimensions – a facet we will be coming back to shortly.

What is networking?

Networking is using your contacts to advance your career. At a practical level it can be applied to the following:

- **Networking for jobs.** As we saw in Chapter 5 you can tap into your contacts to access employment opportunities. Networking, you will remember, was one of the best ways of accessing the elusive invisible market.
- **Networking for promotion.** You can use your networks within organizations to open doors that would otherwise remain shut.
- **Networking for information.** You can tap into your contacts' knowledge banks. For example, you can use your external network to find out how other organizations do things. Or you can see what the outside world is paying people like you.
- **Networking for business.** You can use your contacts as a source of business. For example, people who work for themselves tend to get business from a small circle of contacts – people they know, people who recommend them to others.

Two-way traffic

Networking is a two-way process and seeing it in this way is fundamental to your understanding of how it works. You network someone; they network you back. You ask for a favour (for example, some help with a project); they ask for a favour in return. This two-way traffic is essential to the process and a sign of a good healthy network in operation is where plenty of this to-ing and fro-ing is going on. Conversely, where the traffic is all one-way, at some point the network will wither and die.

Example

Jenny A rings Jane B from time to time to pick her brains. Now, however, Jane B has a problem. Her firm is going into liquidation and she won't have a job in two months' time. On the other hand, Jenny A's firm is expanding hence Jane B rings her to see if she can put in a good word for her. Jenny A, however, is reluctant to do this because she feels it's wrong to pull strings. She tells Jane B, therefore, that she cannot help.

Fine, Jenny A clearly has her principles but, from a networking point of view, she shouldn't be too surprised if she gets the cold shoulder next time she rings Jane B to pick her brains.

Warning

Because networking with people means being prepared to return the favours, it pays to be very careful about whom you include in your circle of contacts. This need for selectivity is a subject we will be returning to again later.

Getting results through networking

Let's introduce another case study at this point so that we can study how networking operates in practice.

Case study 22: David

David is a Product Team Leader and he works for Julie, the Projects Manager. Julie is new to her job and seems intent on stamping her authority on people who work for her. In some cases this results in her being difficult and obstructive – as David found out to his cost a few days ago when he asked for a meeting with her to discuss his next career move. Julie was immediately hostile. She accused him first of wanting to walk out on his team and then said that he could forget career moves until he'd proved to her that he could carry out his current role to her satisfaction.

David is still smarting from this meeting. His next career move was something he'd discussed openly with his old boss, Aaron, and the plan they'd agreed was that David would be transferring to the Costing and Estimating Section as soon as a vacancy became available. With Costing and Estimating experience, David would be a contender for an operational management role in two to three years' time (getting into operational management being David's long-term ambition). Now it seems that Julie's arrival on the scene has put paid to these ambitions. Unfair? Maybe – but what, David asks himself, can he do about it? Julie is the boss after all and once Julie has spoken she rarely, if ever, changes her mind.

At this point many people in David's position would start scanning the job ads and opening up a few options for themselves. David, however, overcame the problem of his difficult boss in another way. Let's go back to the case study to find out what happened.

Case study 22: *continued*

David decides his next step is to have a word with his old boss Aaron. Though Aaron no longer works for the company, David always got on well with him and respects his opinions. If there is a way of dealing with Julie and her intransigence then, in David's view, Aaron is the person most likely to come up with it.

Aaron now works for a firm of management consultants and David fixes up to meet him for a drink one evening after work. Aaron is pleased to see David. He always held him in high regard and he is sorry to hear that he is having problems with Julie. He views Julie as a good manager and he was instrumental in choosing her as his successor, but he is well aware of her ability to dig herself deeper and deeper into holes. Most of all though he sees it as a pity if Julie's stubbornness became the reason for David deciding to pack his bags and leave. The loss would be the company's and, even though Aaron no longer works for the company, he still feels concerned.

Next day Aaron calls Al who is the Divisional Director of his old firm and Julie's immediate boss. Aaron is on good terms with Al and they swap favours from time to time. Has Al heard about the tiff between Julie and David? Al expresses complete surprise. He thought everything was fine on the projects team but, there again, he admits, he is always the last person to find out what's going on. As to Julie blocking David's move to Costing and Estimating, Al is at a loss to understand. Perhaps he is at fault for not briefing Julie more fully on previous discussions about David's future but she only had to ask. Thanking Aaron for giving him the tip-off, Al thinks through his options. Like Aaron, Al has a high opinion of David and views him as a good prospect for the future (someone he would be very sad to lose). What he clearly has to do, therefore, is sort out Julie and get her to back down. This, he realizes, won't be easy.

The important points to extract from David's case study are the following:

- Intentionally or not, David used his external network (his line to Aaron) to get past a difficult boss and advance his career aim.
- The networking only worked because Aaron (and Al) had a good opinion of David.
- Because of his connections, Aaron is a good person to be on networking terms with.

Focusing on the last of these points, networking with people who can influence outcomes for you is important from the point of view of managing your own career and this is a subject we will be returning to shortly.

Key point

Get the power of networking on your side. Pull a few strings if you have to and, where your contacts can influence the outcomes for you, use them.

Notepad

The image you put across in your day-to-day dealings with people determines to a large extent your ability to develop effective networks. Put another way, no one will want to network with you if they have reservations about you, just as you won't want to network with people that don't measure up to your standards (the point we discussed a few pages back). This link between networking and your lifelong interview is an important one and we shall be exploring it further in the next chapter.

Evaluating opportunities

Communicating your ideas clearly and letting silent bargaining power do the work for you will hopefully culminate in you getting the result you want, that is, the realization of your aim. However, sometimes your employer comes back to you with an idea different from the one you proposed. The leverage worked but not in the way you expected. Another case study will help to illustrate the kind of dilemma you could face.

Case study 23: Craig

Craig works as a buyer for an office equipment and stationery supplier. He is 28 and has been in this job for the past four years.

Craig's main gripe is his salary. He feels he is not adequately recompensed for the responsibilities he carries and he has recently made these views known to his boss, the General Manager. Yesterday, however, the General Manager called him into her office and, to his complete surprise, she offered him a job running a new retail outlet that will come on stream in six months' time. The salary mentioned was a big improvement on his current package and he would also qualify for a company car. What did Craig think? Craig wasn't too sure. He'd always seen his future in buying and, other than the issue of his pay, he was perfectly happy in his present job.

Putting the art of the possible into practice

Clearly Craig's silent bargaining power had some impact, but it didn't get the result he wanted, namely staying in the job of buyer but on a better salary. His company came up with the better salary but in an entirely different job role and one that Craig hadn't considered previously. What should be read into this?

- A problem, perhaps, in paying Craig more as a buyer (possibly a problem of differentials with other members of staff).
- As a consequence, the possibility that the aim wasn't realizable.
- An indicator that the leverage triggered by Craig's silent bargaining power worked (his boss felt moved to come up with some positive gesture).

Clearly Craig has to decide whether to say yes or no to his boss's offer and this may be difficult for him. The pathway to a better salary is open but, if he takes it, it means ditching his cherished ambition of making his career in buying. What should he do?

- First, put a few serious questions to himself about his ambition to stay in buying. For example, is it baggage and, if so, how important is it to him (really)? Or could it be that he's falling into the trap of having ambitions that are too narrow and rigid?
- Second, consider the art of the possible. The job managing the retail outlet is there on a plate waiting for him to snap it up whereas getting a better paid job as an office equipment buyer may prove to be a hard aim to achieve.
- Third, if he wants to advance his salary in buying it looks like he will have to pursue his ambitions elsewhere.

Questions and answers

Silent bargaining power doesn't work for me

Q *I'm 22, recently graduated and I've taken a job working for a firm of investment advisers. Since starting, however, I've discovered that the salary I'm being paid is way below what graduates working in this industry would normally expect to earn, hence I took up my concerns with one of the partners. Sad to say, however, this got me nowhere. The partner made some noises about salaries being reviewed at the end of the year and that was that: the matter was closed. What I want to know is why my silent bargaining power didn't have more impact. Or could it be that my firm doesn't really value my worth?*

A Some organizations conspicuously undervalue the input of people who work for them but, in your case, a far more likely explanation for your lack of success is your newness to the firm. Remember this is about value expressed in terms of the damage you would inflict on the business if you decided to leave. As a beginner, any damage would by definition be minimal, hence you don't have much in the way of silent bargaining power. Console yourself with the thought that your turn comes later (when you've added to your value by adding to your skills and experience).

Too long in the job

Q *I'm on a very poor salary for the work I do but I guess I don't have much in the way of silent bargaining power because I'm in my fifties with over 25 years' service with my company, meaning no one would ever take the threat of me leaving seriously. Is this the price I've paid for staying too long in the job? Is it simply a case of plodding on until I'm old enough to pick up my pension?*

A What you need to consider is that with 25 years' service you've probably got all kinds of knowledge and experience locked up inside your head – knowledge and experience that would be sorely missed if you ever decided to leave suddenly. However, in common with a lot of people with long service, where you fall down is with your credibility: everyone sees you as welded into the fabric of the organization and, as you rightly say, no one seriously entertains the thought of you ever walking out. What to do? Our suggestion is to take the bull by the horns. Tell your company that you feel there's a connection between your long service and your poor pay. Tell them too that it would be unfortunate both for them and for you if you had to resolve your pay problem by going out and shopping around for something better, but emphasize at the same time that this is the last thing you would ever want to do. What you will achieve by having this dialogue is to send out a coded message that the idea of going after another job is not something that frightens you. In this way – and without making threats – you will be removing the impression that you're part of the furniture (the impression that's undermining your credibility). Will it work? It may or may not. If it doesn't then another way would be to try using your internal networks along the lines suggested in this chapter. People with long service usually have excellent internal networks. In short, now could be the time for pulling a few strings.

What's wrong with blackmail?

Q *On the subject of silent bargaining power I've seen a number of people in my organization get exactly what they want (a rise normally) by threatening to leave. In this context what is so bad about blackmail? If it works why not use it?*

A People who enjoy most success with blackmail are usually people with quite formidable stores of silent bargaining power – for example, people in sales with lots of valuable contacts or people with creative skills such as designers. Why do we advise against blackmail? First, for the reason given in the text that employers don't always respond to threats in the way you expect them to (if you threaten to resign you could find they snatch your hand off). Second, blackmail tends to be a one shot game. You can use it once but if you try it again no one takes you quite so seriously the second time. More to the point, the cumulative effect is an ever-increasing dent in your credibility which over time will serve to undermine your bargaining power completely.

Career aim on track then nothing happened

Q *I had a very congenial meeting with my boss about my ambition to move from my present head office position in marketing to a job running one of our operational divisions. He even agreed with me that this would be an excellent career move and that my experience in marketing would make me a good candidate for taking on any division where the main item in the brief was to manage change. Six months have now lapsed since this meeting took place and, every time I have tried to raise the subject again, my boss's manner has been evasive. Where do I proceed from here?*

A Opportunities to move round in organizations don't come up overnight and you should allow for this. On the other hand, your boss's evasiveness could indicate he is having trouble pressing your case with people above him or some other event is looming on the corporate horizon that is taking precedence over staff development. Our suggestion would be to have one last go at pinning your boss down and, if you are greeted by further evasiveness, to set a time limit on 'something happening' along the lines we've described in this chapter. At this next meeting with your boss it would do no harm to voice your concerns about lack of progress just to see what reaction you get.

Offered promotion but with no increase in salary

Q *After making a bid for promotion onto our board of management, I was finally successful at the end of last year. What I discovered to my dismay, however, was that the promotion wasn't accompanied by an increase in salary. I know that other members of the board of management are paid considerably more than me and I feel this is extremely unfair to the point where I am considering telling the Chief Executive what to do with his promotion. Any advice?*

A It could be that the company is seeing how you perform in your new position before moving you onto a higher salary (one comparable with that of your peers). Otherwise, see getting your salary raised to an acceptable level as your next aim (a case of taking your aims one at a time). With this in mind, smile sweetly and give the new job your best shot so that all the time you're building up your silent bargaining power ready for when you need it to work for you.

Summary

As part of managing your own career you should be in no doubt at all that the onus rests on you for making sure your employer understands:

- you
- where you are coming from
- what you are seeking to achieve.

The fact that your boss is too busy, too introspective, too indolent, too remote or too anything else is largely irrelevant. This is your career. Look after it. Steer it in directions you want it to go in and never leave it to others to do the steering for you. Never leave it to chance either.

08

moving into the future

In this chapter you will learn:
- what it takes to be good at managing your own career
- the importance of building effective professional networks
- how to go on being successful.

In this final chapter we are going to pull together the lessons in the book and provide you with a blueprint for moving into the future with the management of your career. We are going to look at:

- Perfecting a winning image – building on your lifelong interview and using it to access the cream of what the market for your talents has to offer.
- Creating effective networks – developing your circle of contacts to include more of the right people.
- Staying on-line with the job market – abandoning the stop-start approach to sourcing opportunities and being aware at all times of what is out there for you.
- Lifelong learning – adding to your value and bolstering your silent bargaining power as part of a continuous improvement process.

Perfecting a winning image

At several points through the book we have touched on the importance of the image you project in your day-to-day dealings with people. In particular, we have seen:

- How a person-perfect/work-perfect image is essential if you want to access the cream of the jobs by getting onto headhunters' networks.
- How your image matters when it comes to striking up networking relationships with people.
- How people who know you have a big part to play in moving your career forward.
- How a flaw in your character when transmitted to others can work to your detriment.
- How putting over a good image plays a large part in the success of people who work for themselves or on short-term assignments.

For these reasons we have encouraged you to view the quality of the image you project as an everyday challenge and one you should be constantly focusing your attention on. With this aim in mind, we coined the term 'lifelong interview' – it's like putting on your best performance when you go for a job interview except in this case you're doing it all the time.

What does this mean in practice? Let's take another case study to illustrate one of the hardest parts of the lifelong interview to get right.

Case study 24: Joanne

Joanne has recently been through a bad patch in her career, but three months ago she was successful in landing a job with a reputable firm of chartered accountants. Immediately on starting she was assigned to Ros to show her the ropes and this went well – the two of them got on very well and soon they were meeting up socially and going out to clubs together.

However, it was during the course of one of these outings that Joanne let it slip out to Ros that she'd been in trouble in her last job. She'd passed on some information about a client to a third party and, when the Managing Partner got to hear about it, he went ballistic. In the end she was let off with a severe reprimand but the incident effectively put paid to her promotion chances.

Two days after this conversation with Ros, Joanne's boss Kelly asked her to step into the office. She'd heard a whisper, she said, that Joanne wasn't to be trusted with confidential information and asked if it was true that this had been a problem with her last firm. Caught off guard, Joanne admitted that she'd once made an error of judgement but, the more she tried to explain, the more it sounded as though she had something to hide. Kelly, she could tell, wasn't happy with her answer and, although she didn't say a lot, Joanne knew that the interview had left a question mark in her mind.

Keep your flaws to yourself

In any organization nothing functions quite so well as the grapevine and secrets, once shared with work colleagues, don't remain secrets for very long. In Joanne's case the fact that she'd got herself into serious hot water at some point in the past stood a good chance of staying under wraps until she chose to confide in Ros. Effectively she scotched the chance to lay the past to rest and start her lifelong interview all over again in her new firm.

A difficulty for all of us is that the relationships we form with people we meet through our work often do turn into close personal friendships. Then it becomes much harder, of course, to stop the odd indiscretion slipping out; the odd glimpse into some darker episode in our past. The result? Our lifelong interview is blown off course and we're left with the task of picking up the pieces.

> **Key point**
>
> When it comes to building professional networks, don't:
>
> - do as Joanne did and succumb to the temptation of getting too close;
> - let out anything that could put you in a bad light.
>
> We've all got flaws and the trick is to keep them to ourselves.

Leaving jobs on good terms

Whenever you leave a job there is always the temptation to 'say a few words'. You can get the various niggles you've had over the years off your chest, and you can even tell the boss a few home truths because it doesn't seem to matter any more. In a few days you'll be off and you won't be coming back. As far as you're concerned this particular chapter in your life is closed.

What happens in these brief ventings of your spleen is that your lifelong interview falls apart in the space of a few sentences. The difficulty for you then is when at some point in the future your ex-boss is asked to pass an opinion on you – possibly to someone who is contemplating making you a good offer or who wants to know what you're like to do business with.

The message here is to learn to bite your tongue if you feel the urge to air your opinions more freely as you approach the point of leaving. Instead:

- Find it in yourself somewhere to say a few nice things about your time with the organization (even if the words stick in your throat).
- Complete any outstanding work and ensure a smooth hand-over of responsibilities to your successor.
- Offer to be available to answer any queries that arise after you've left ('just give me a call').
- Work out your notice in full and co-operate with any requests your employer makes – for example, to return keys or any company property you are holding.

Visibility

Having a good image is all well and good, but it won't get you very far if no one is aware of it. This brings us onto visibility or *projecting* your image to people who count.

The key to understanding visibility is that, if you want it to work, it has to associate you with the right things. To show what we mean by this here are two examples of visibility, one good and one bad.

Example A: Honest Joe

Checking his salary slip one month, Joe notices that he's been overpaid for the number of hours' overtime he's worked. Joe realizes that the chances of the error being picked up are slight. Nevertheless he goes to see the Human Resources Manager and declares the overpayment.

Example B: Idle Jack

Jack is late for work most mornings of the week. Unfortunately for Jack his office happens to be just along the corridor from the Managing Director's.

In Example A the visibility Honest Joe creates by going to see the Human Resources Manager associates him with something good (personal integrity). Conversely in Example B we have someone whose visibility associates him with something bad (poor timekeeping). It is important to understand that these images of someone honest and upright or someone who can't be bothered to get out of bed in the morning are images that tend to stick to the point where they're hard to shift.

Creating effective networks

Part of moving into the future by managing your own career is developing your professional network to include more and more of the right people. In turn this means:

- becoming increasingly selective about the people you enter into networking relationships with;
- shedding anyone from your network who no longer measures up.

Why compact is beautiful

You may recall a point we made earlier on about there being no virtue whatsoever in getting onto networking terms with an ever-increasing number of people. What matters with a professional network isn't the headcount but the way that you use it and, like any good machine, a professional network benefits from being kept in good running order – meaning the more you use it, the better it functions. Conversely, if you don't keep your network in good running order then pretty soon it rusts up and becomes useless. So, for example, if Tom phones Dick for help and information on a regular basis and if Dick phones back for help and information on an equally regular basis in return, it's a good sign that Tom's network is working well. If, on the other hand, years go by with no contact between Tom and Dick, the opposite applies. If Tom has a need to phone Dick for a favour, he may find it awkward for the simple reasons that it has been such a long time since the two of them last spoke. Alternatively, Dick may have moved on and Tom may no longer have his number.

Seen in this context, a compact well-functioning network is preferable by far to one which you can't handle because of the sheer number of people. An over-populated network will beat you and you will end up not seeing any of the benefits.

Applying selectivity to networks

Consistent with the aim of keeping your professional network compact and manageable, you need to prune it from time to time and get rid of any people who no longer come up to standard. In doing this, you need to bear in mind that continuing to have networking relationships with people who have become unsatisfactory will sooner or later pose problems for you as our next case study illustrates

---

Case study 25: Simon and Jill

Simon works for a well-known software house where he is highly regarded and in line for promotion. One day Simon is approached by Jill who he has known for a long time and who helped him get his first job after leaving university. Jill, it seems, has gone freelance and she is looking for work. She wants Simon to put in a good word for her with his boss. Simon, for his part, has grave reservations about doing this. He knows that Jill has become very unreliable and deadlines mean nothing to her (he suspects this was the reason why she lost her last job). Also Simon is only too aware that by recommending Jill he will be putting his own reputation on the line. Ideally he would like to tell Jill he can't help but understandably he finds this difficult.

Simon is spot on in his reading of the situation. If, on the strength of his recommendation, his firm offers Jill some work and if she subsequently lets them down, then some of the resulting fall-out will come down on his head. The upshot? A dent in his hitherto well-managed image. Saying he can't help may be difficult for Simon but clearly this is something he must do either by being honest with Jill or by thinking up some excuse.

Key point

Don't fudge when it comes to picking people to network with and don't allow your judgement to be undermined by misplaced loyalty to long-standing friends. Deselect people you don't have confidence in any more and remember that, as far as your network is concerned, there is no such thing as life membership.

How to rid your network of people who have become unsatisfactory

Though the process sounds potentially painful, deselecting people who have become unsatisfactory often involves little more than turning the principles of good networking around and applying them in reverse. Remember the two-way flow on which all networks thrive? Once you stop using a contact the automatic tendency is for the flow coming back to you to dry up – a case of don't phone them and they won't phone you.

Widening your circle of contacts

As you advance in your career you will come into contact with an increasing number of people who can influence outcomes for you – examples are:

• **People at the top:** people who can make big differences to the pace at which your career moves forward.

- **External contacts:** people outside your own organization who can help you source jobs or put your name in the hat when interesting opportunities arise.
- **Well-connected people:** typically people who move round in business circles, such as consultants and professional advisers.
- **Headhunters:** people whose business it is to have connections and who can put you in touch with some of the best opportunities that the job market has to offer.
- **Professional contacts:** people in the same line of work as you; people you meet through bodies such as professional associations.

All of the above have the potential to be able to influence the outcomes for you, hence, as a good manager of your own career, you should be actively seeking to include them in your circle of contacts.

Getting headhunted

Because headhunting is focused on the top end of the job market there are enormous benefits for you if, as part of your plan for the future, you can make yourself a target for headhunters' approaches. How do you do this? First and foremost you need to appreciate that, with big future billings at stake, headhunters don't take chances with people. Most of their business is obtained by reputation so the last thing they want is to be known as the search organization that landed one of their clients with a senior executive who was not a success.

So what happens? Headhunters play safe. They confine their attentions to people who can project a person-perfect and work-perfect image – thus explaining why people who are good at their lifelong interview are those who go on to become targets for approach.

Getting yourself headhunted doesn't stop there, however. To get your name on a professional search consultant's call list, someone somewhere has to put in the right word for you – illustrating, again, the key role played by people you know in moving your career forward in desirable directions. How does this work? Here is an example of a typical headhunting assignment.

Example

XXX Plastic Components is looking for a new Managing Director for one of its subsidiaries and they approach ZZZ & Partners, a leading firm of executive search consultants. A specification is drawn up and ZZZ are briefed to find someone with a proven track record of running a successful medium-sized plastics company. ZZZ start the assignment by running through their list of contacts in the plastics industry.

One of the names that they pull out is Bill – a plastics specialist they placed with a client about 12 months ago. Bill has been in the plastics industry all his life and, because he's moved around, he knows who's who and whether they're any good. Can Bill recommend anyone for the job with their client? Bill asks for 24 hours to think about it, although two names (Jake and Anna) have already sprung to mind.

Jake and Anna have both had the right experience (running successful plastics businesses) and both would probably be interested in making a move. Jake, however, bothers him. Good businessman he may be, but he has problems in his private life and, at points in the past, he has allowed these problems to affect his work. Bill is acutely aware that ZZZ will make checks on anyone he puts forward and Jake's inconsistencies will be bound to surface, meaning his own reputation as a judge of character will be at stake. No, Bill decides, he'll stick to recommending Anna. His relationship with ZZZ is important to him. He could be looking to make a move himself soon, meaning he'd need to call on ZZZ's services.

Key points to pick out from this example are the following:

- how headhunters operate by tapping into other people's networks;
- how Bill's insight into Jake's character worked against him;
- how Bill was motivated by his own self-interest (keeping on the right side of the headhunters);
- how Jake would have fared better if he'd managed to keep the difficulties in his private life to himself;
- how Jake is none the wiser to any of these events (the fact that he didn't get an approach and the reasons for it are never made known to him).

Apart from re-emphasizing some of the earlier messages in the book, this example serves to demonstrate the link between being a target for approach and:

- good image management;
- good networking practice.

Get these right and you will find that your ability to connect with the best that the job market has to offer will increase many times over.

Staying on-line with the job market

Most people engage with the market for their talents only when they have to. Their job comes under threat; they are passed by for promotion; the pay rise they expected doesn't materialize and they're forced into seeing what else is out there for them. They shoot off several job applications, register with firms of recruitment consultants, send out copies of their CVs and, sooner or later, something suitable comes along. But what happens next?

They disengage from the job market immediately and usually stay disengaged for quite a long time (until the next wave of disaffection sweeps over them). The problem with this stop–start approach is illustrated by our next case study.

Case study 26: Kent

Kent works in the civil engineering industry and he has been on the job market three times in his life – each time when civil engineering was going through a recession and his job was under threat. The result was that he found jobs hard to come by – partly because of the state of the industry and partly because there were many other people like him shopping around for something more secure.

What Kent hasn't seen, of course, is the market for his talents in more buoyant times. The result is that his perception of the market is a distorted one and, as a consequence, his expectations are set low. The bottom line for people like Kent is that they underachieve.

Abandoning the stop–start approach

A further problem with the stop–start approach is that, every time you try to engage with the market for your talents, you are left with having to make a completely cold start. It takes time for your experience to build up. Equally it takes time for the true extent of the market to unfold. Time, of course, isn't always on your side, meaning:

• you take the first decent offer that turns up;
• the true extent of the market is never revealed to you.

What you need to do instead, of course, is have an ongoing view of what the market for your talents has to offer. How do you achieve this?

• Stay in contact with the market by keeping your eye on ads in newspapers and journals and on websites. Apply for a job once in a while.
• Stay on the books of selected recruitment consultants. In this way keep in touch with the invisible market.
• Keep working on your networks. Let your contacts know you're always in the market for good opportunities.
• Keep working on your lifelong interview. Strive to project the person-perfect/work-perfect image and in this way make yourself a target for approach.
• Encourage headhunters to keep calling you. Do this by never putting up the shutters to them. Always hear out what they have to say.

The advantages of the approach outlined above are as follows:

• You won't be in the position of having to make cold starts. You will have the market at your finger tips, so that should the need arise to access it quickly, you won't have to wait for the opportunities to unfold.
• You will find out if your skills are not in line with what the market wants. With time on your side you will be able to rectify any areas of potential disadvantage.
• You will be able to practise and perfect your interview skills.
• Who knows, you may even be offered a good job!

Key point

The world we live in is governed by uncertainty and no one truly knows what's around the next corner. For this reason, good career management means having all of your options open all of the time.

Lifelong learning

Lifelong learning has different meanings for different people. We use this term to describe the process of continuously adding value to yourself in order to boost your silent bargaining power and enhance your capacity to exert more and more leverage. The quest to acquire new skills, more knowledge, a greater range of experience should be seen, in other words, as an everyday part of your life and something you should focus on constantly as part of a plan to achieve personal betterment through the advancement of your career.

Develop areas of expertise

It hardly needs saying that if you can become the world's leading authority in your field your career opportunities will have practically no bounds. Yet there is scope for all of us to develop areas of expertise that will add substantially to our silent bargaining power. Take the example of Naomi. Naomi is a PA who developed her IT skills to a high level of proficiency so that she is now the person in her firm to whom everyone turns when the need arises to sort out problems with the systems. Everyone says 'Where would we be without Naomi?', and this state of affairs means, of course, that Naomi has accumulated enormous amounts of silent bargaining power. As a consequence her employers, if they have any sense, will go to great lengths to keep her happy and, if they don't, there will be plenty of takers for her on the outside job market.

No one told Naomi to become an IT expert. As it happened, the subject interested her but the motivation to study at home, fathom out snags and persuade her employers to let her go on courses came entirely from her. The rest was simply a matter of 'willing hands'. If there was a problem she got involved. If someone needed help, she was always there to provide it. Most importantly, she never once uttered words such as 'Sorry, I'm too busy' or 'I only do what I'm paid to do.' And what happened? Over a period of time people in her firm discovered that it was easier to say 'Ask Naomi' than it was to sort out the problem for themselves. Soon a state of dependency developed and, in terms of her silent bargaining power, it was Naomi who reaped the benefits.

Acquire a scarce skill

This is the business of taking the development of expertise to its extreme. A feature of recent years has been chronic skills shortages in certain sectors of the economy fuelled, in some cases, by rapid growth and, in others, by under-investment in training (or a combination of both). Possessors of scarce skills can virtually call their own tune when it comes to determining items such as their pay or the terms and conditions under which they work. What's more, recruiting people with scarce skills is often done by making approaches to them (either directly or through a professional headhunter). The result (as in all situations where demand exceeds supply many times over) is that individuals can largely dictate their own packages – needless to say, a very envious position to be in.

So if your lifelong learning can encompass acquiring a scarce skill then this is a very desirable aim for you to pursue. Take note, those of you who are contemplating a change of career: if you can move into one of these scarce skill areas then your future is practically guaranteed.

Questions and answers

moving into the future 08

How do I start a networking relationship?

Q *I want to network with someone who doesn't know me very well so how do I make a start? Is it a case of introducing myself and exchanging business cards or is there anything else I need to do first?*

A Step one, always, is to ensure that the person you're intending to network with passes the tests as far as inclusion in your circle of contacts is concerned. Perhaps this person doesn't know you very well, but could you vouch for his or her trustworthiness and reliability? The cue here is to form a view of people over periods of time *before* you enter into networking relationships with them and only to proceed if you are satisfied with what you've seen. How do you start? Try doing them a good turn – for example, provide them with some information that would be useful to them. In networking terms this gets the two-way traffic moving and you can follow up by asking for some minor favour in return. If all goes well then you will soon be able to confer full membership of your network on your new contact.

Networking and confidentiality

Q *I take the point about always keeping my ear to the ground for good opportunities but I would be concerned about spreading the word around my circle of contacts for the simple reason that my boss could get to hear that I'm looking to make a move. Any comment?*

A Your question highlights two of the main difficulties to networking: first, it tends to access quite small worlds and, second, within those small worlds, walls tend to have ears. The answer? Don't network with anyone you don't trust: this includes the kind of people who get a kick out of gossip and tittle-tattle. As a further control, make it clear to your contacts that you wish your interest in good opportunities to be treated in strictest confidence and not to be discussed with any third parties without your prior knowledge and approval. At the same time emphasize the difficulties for you if your wider ambitions should ever leak back to the wrong ears.

Summary

Moving into the future with managing your own career means:

- perfecting the skills you have acquired already;
- keeping yourself positioned so that the world is at your fingertips and you can enjoy the best of what the market for your talents has to offer.

Careers today lack certainty and stability and, for this reason, they can appear 'difficult'. Where they do score, however, is with their richness and diversity – a richness and diversity that is very much a reflection of the modern world and one that wasn't there 20 or 30 years ago. What this means, for example, is that you can spend the first fifteen years of your career climbing the corporate ladder but then, as your ambitions change, you can try something completely different – working for yourself perhaps or embarking on an entirely new career. Later on you may decide to change directions again, the key point being that the opportunities are there providing you are poised and equipped to take advantage of them. This is what managing your own career is all about.

index